Cheese Cookery

Doris McFerran Townsend

CONTENTS

ANOTHER BEST-SELLING VOLUME FROM H.P. BOOKS

Publisher: Helen Fisher; Editor: Carroll Latham; Art Director: Don Burton;
Book Design: Tom Jakeway; Typography: Cindy Coatsworth, Joanne Nociti, Kris Spitler;
Line Drawings: Pat O'Dell, Tom Jakeway; Food Stylist: Janet Pittman;
Photography: George deGennaro Studios.

Published by H.P. Books, P.O. Box 5367, Tucson, AZ 85703 602/888-2150
ISBN 0-89586-039-2
Library of Congress Catalog Card Number 80-80167

Cover Photo: Cheese Display, see page 5 for legend

Wide World Of Cheese

According to legend, cheese was discovered by a shepherd boy about 4000 B.C. The boy left his milk pouch in the sun and set off on his daily rounds. When he returned, heat combined with enzymes in the pouch had coagulated the milk. The boy tasted it gingerly. Joy! Cheese had come into being!

For hundreds of years all cheese was more or less alike. Flavor differences depended on the kind of *milk* used to make a particular cheese. All cheese begins with milk—from goats, cows, reindeer, camels, mares or any lactating animal—and all cheesemaking begins with separation of *curds*, or solid matter, from *whey*, or liquid. Early cheeses were usually *fresh*, or *unripened*, as our *cream cheese* and *cottage cheese* are today. If they were strong in flavor and aroma it was because they had been around too long. About 900 B.C., imaginative cheesemakers began to use *enzymes* from thistles, figs and assorted weeds to *ripen* or *cure* their products. They learned to heat milk and to press curds to separate them from whey more completely than simple draining. They began to stir curds and *comb* them for better texture, and to salt, oil or otherwise treat outsides of cheeses so they would ripen rather than spoil as they *aged*. One adventurous fellow added rye breadcrumbs to his cheese, let it ripen in a dark cave and previewed arrival of French *bleus*, Danish *blues*, *Wensleydales*, *Roqueforts* and *Stiltons*. Monks of the Middle Ages found time to develop many wines and cheeses. From cloisters came such triumphs as *Pont l'Evêque*, *Port Salut* and many more. The making of cheese spread throughout most of the known world—everywhere but the Orient. Probably because they did not use milk in any form, no one in the Far East discovered cheese nor is it in common use today in Oriental cuisines. Today there are 700 to 2000 kinds of cheese, depending on which authority you believe. France alone boasts 500 kinds, the United States 200.

Some cheeses are quite common. Others are rare—and expensive. One example is *crottin de Chavignol*, a small cheese made of salted goat's milk. It makes a brief yearly appearance in Paris markets and demands a high price.

Whatever your taste, there is a cheese to suit it. Flavors, aromas and moisture content range from mild, delicate and soft to strong, heady and hard-as-a-rock. All these differences are determined by treatment of the curd, addition of friendly bacteria or molds and conditions under which cheese is *ripened*.

Making Cheese

Cheesemaking may have begun as an accident, but it soon became a common household activity. Cheese not only supplied the family with a nutritious food, but used milk that would have otherwise spoiled. Household cheesemaking soon moved from kitchen to factory. Today dairymen collect milk in large sterile vats for cooling. Cooled milk is transported in large sterile tank trucks to cheese factories. At the factories, most cheeses go through a fairly standard procedure.

Starting with Milk—Fresh milk is scientifically tested and heat treated. Fat content is adjusted, depending on the kind of cheese to be made. Milk is heated a second time and pumped into vats.

Various Additions—Coloring is used in some cheeses. For a golden-yellow cheese, a vegetable coloring of the desired shade may be added. *Starter*, a pure culture of micro-organisms that firms curd particles and begins development of the characteristics of that particular cheese, is added. Then *rennet extract* is added to coagulate curd particles into a custard-like mass.

Cutting and Cooking—After the curd reaches a custard-like firmness, it is cut into small cubes with a device resembling a large comb. Whey begins to separate from the curds. Curds and whey are heated together to the required cooking temperature for the kind of cheese being made. Further cooking firms the curds and speeds separation from the whey.

Removing Whey—A simple draining process—accomplished mechanically in modern cheese factories by centrifugal force—removes the whey, leaving curds behind.

Salting Curds—Salt may be added to curds at this point or after the cheese is *pressed.* The amount of salt and when it is added to the curds have a definite effect on the type of cheese produced.

Pressing and Ripening or Curing—Curds are weighed, then pressed into *forms*, such as wooden *hoops* or metal *cylinders*, to produce solid blocks of cheese. The pressed cheese is ripened or *cured* in a temperature-controlled area to develop the desired texture and flavor.

Cheese Families

Cheeses can be divided into broad categories based on *ripening*. Some cheeses are *fresh*, meant to be eaten as soon as they are made, without aging. Others are ripened for varying lengths of time. Within each of these two broad classifications are many kinds of cheeses, and under each general kind are many variations. This accounts for the almost infinite variety of cheeses you see in a cheese store.

Fresh or Unripened Cheeses—These have soft textures and mild flavors. In making fresh cheeses, coagulation of the curd is started by adding lactic acid rather than rennet, or by combining lactic acid with a small amount of rennet.

Cream cheese was first developed in the United States by combining whole milk and cream—which was then pasteurized and coagulated. Early cream cheese was poured into cloth bags and pressed to expel the whey, but a method of separation by centrifugal force was perfected in 1945. This produces a fine-textured, smooth-bodied cheese that keeps much better than cream cheese made by the old method.

Neufchâtel, spelled *Neuchâtel* in Switzerland, is similar to cream cheese, but has a lower fat content. It also has a mild flavor and smooth, creamy texture.

Cottage cheese is made from skim milk coagulated by lactic acid. Sometimes a small amount of rennet is added. Firmed large or small curds are heated in whey, then whey is drained off and curds are washed and salted. Cottage cheese may be purchased dry or creamed with a mixture of cream and milk.

Ricotta is a whey cheese and will be talked about with other whey cheeses. *Mozzarella* and its close relative *scamorze* are made like the *provolone* family but are actually firm, unripened cheeses.

All fresh cheeses mix well with other ingredients, such as herbs, minced vegetables, olives or chopped sausage. You can flavor cheeses at home or purchase them already mixed with flavoring ingredients.

Ripened or Aged Cheeses—Each cheese in this classification is made within its own range of time and temperature and ripened under its own conditions. This gives each cheese its unique flavor, texture and appearance. Some are aged as long as

24 months. The longer a cheese is ripened, the sharper the flavor becomes. Short ripening time results in a mild-flavored cheese.

Ripened cheeses fall into family groups, and there may be few or many individual kinds of cheese in each group. Most ripened cheeses originated in Europe. Today they are manufactured by similar methods in many countries.

Cheddar is the most popular group of cheeses in English speaking countries. Like all varieties of natural cheese, Cheddars are made as described above. What sets them apart is the treatment at the whey-draining step. A process called *cheddaring* allows curds to knit together as they are turned and piled to expel whey. This develops Cheddar's characteristic body and texture. After cheddaring, the flattened slab is cut into smaller pieces and placed in hoops or molds. Cheese labeled *Cheddar* is usually golden-yellow and available in mild, mellow, sharp and extra-sharp flavors. An uncolored or white Cheddar is also available.

Some members of the Cheddar family, such as *Colby*, are stirred instead of being allowed to knit, giving it a more open texture. The drained curd is washed with cold water, resulting in a higher moisture content and milder flavor.

Dutch cheeses are semisoft to hard sweet-curd cheeses made from cow's milk. Their characteristic milky, nut-like flavor varies with age. They are shaped in hardwood or metal molds. Some Dutch cheeses are flavored with cumin, caraway or other spices.

Curd of *provolone cheeses* is *spun*. The curd is placed in hot water or whey until a stringy mass forms. This mass is stretched, much as taffy is pulled, then molded to the desired size and shape. It is soaked in brine to salt it, after which it may or may not be smoked.

Swiss cheeses are characterized by the *eyes* or *holes* which develop during ripening. Today *Swiss* means holes and flavor reminiscent of *Emmentaler* cheeses, not Switzerland. Holes are caused by *propionic acid bacteria* that produce carbon dioxide bubbles in the curd mass. They also give Swiss cheese its sweet, nut-like flavor.

Blue-veined cheeses originated in many countries. All are characterized by veins of blue-green mold which contribute to the distinctive flavor of each cheese. During manufacture of the cheeses, *penicillium mold* is mixed with curds while in the vat or when placed in molds or hoops. Molds or hoops are removed after 24 hours. The cheese is salted for about 7 days under conditions simulating temperature and humidity of famous caves where *Roquefort* cheese is ripened. After one week, the cheese is pierced to allow air to penetrate. Air is essential for mold growth. The cheese is then ripened approximately five months.

Hard-grating cheeses are ripened for a long time under conditions that develop flavor and texture. Their hard, granular texture makes them ideal for grating.

Surface-Ripened Cheeses—All cheeses in this group are ripened by a bacteria or mold culture grown on the surface. Enzymes produced by this growth penetrate the cheese and cause the characteristic flavor and texture of each variety. *Camembert* and *Brie* are surface-ripened cheeses with authoritative but subtle flavors.

Whey Cheeses—Because whey is a byproduct of cheesemaking, these are technically not cheeses. Best known of this group is *ricotta*, a fresh cheese. Ricotta was originally produced by coagulation of the albumen portion of whey. Today it is made from a combination of whey and whole or skim milk. *Gjetost* and *primost* are prepared by condensing whey and adding a small amount of fat. *Sapsago* is produced by acid coagulation of a combination of whey, buttermilk and skim milk.

Process Cheeses—In the early 1900's a young door-to-door cheese salesman began experimenting, hoping to make cheese that would overcome one of the food's greatest drawbacks, its short life. He accomplished his purpose and produced a cheese with very good keeping qualities. Consumers casually call it *American* process cheese but its correct name is *pasteurized process cheese*.

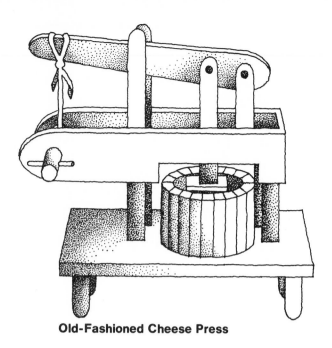

Old-Fashioned Cheese Press

Process cheese starts with a blend of natural cheeses heated with an *emulsifier*. Pasteurization halts aging of the natural cheese, giving a product with consistent flavor, body, texture and excellent keeping qualities. It melts readily and smoothly and is often used in cooking. Pasteurized process cheese further treated with whey or milk results in *pastueurized process cheese food*. With additional moisture, it becomes *pasteurized process cheese spread*—often flavored with olives, pimientos, pickles or spices.

Serving Cheese

Cheese to be eaten out of hand is best when served at room temperature when character and flavor are at their optimum. Remove cheese from the refrigerator 30 minutes to one hour before serving and let it come to room temperature. This is not true of *cottage* cheese, *Neufchâtel* and *cream* cheese. These are best when chilled. Take them from the refrigerator five to ten minutes before serving.

COOKING WITH CHEESE
When you cook with cheese, remember two key words—*low* and *slow*. Cheese cannot tolerate quick cooking at high temperatures. In making a cheese sauce, the cheese—usually shredded or grated—is added last and the sauce is stirred over low heat only until the cheese is melted. If you top a casserole with cheese, add it during the last five or ten minutes of cooking. Bake casseroles containing cheese at a temperature no higher than 375°F (190°C). When broiling cheese, place the food several inches from the heat source. Broil only until the cheese is well-softened.

How To Choose Cheese

If you are a cheese fancier, you probably don't need a buying guide. But if your horizons are bounded by Cheddar, Swiss, cottage and cream, it's time you got started on the big cheese adventure.

The best way to begin is to go to a cheese shop and sample, sample, sample! If you can find a proprietor who started the business because he really dotes on cheese, he can teach you more in an hour or so than you'd gather from a week of reading. Poking around in a supermarket's cheese department—no matter how large and well-stocked—won't be much help. What you'll see are a lot of pretty wrappings without a clue to the character inside them. Here is a guide to some of the world's great cheeses you'll want to sample.

CHEDDAR & ITS RELATIVES

These fairly hard cheeses have assertive flavors and somewhat crumbly textures. To begin a Cheddar sampling, look for wedges of golden *New York Cheddar* with a black-wax protective coating or paler, more moist, *Vermont Cheddar*. Or try Cheddar in foil-wrapped sticks. These are marked *mild*, *mellow*, *sharp* and *extra sharp* to guide you. *Monterey Jack*—or simply *jack*—is cream-colored and more moist. Golden-yellow *Colby* and *Longhorn* are moist, mild-flavored Cheddars. Both are *stirred* Cheddars. Longhorn is usually cut in round slices.

SWISS CHEESES

Emmentaler is the original Swiss cheese. This marvelous cheese with a sweet nut-like flavor comes from Switzerland in large wheels, from which your cheese merchant will happily cut a wedge for you. *Gruyère* comes from Switzerland or France. It has smaller holes than regular Swiss and an excellent texture. It's the classic Swiss cheese for cooking. Because some surface ripening is allowed to develop, it has a somewhat sharper flavor than Emmentaler. Much of the Gruyère sold in the United States is pasteurized process cheese made by combining natural Emmentaler and Gruyère. It is sold in packages containing individually wrapped wedges and is not at all what you would get if you asked for Gruyère in Switzerland or in a very good cheese shop. *Appenzeller*, another Swiss from Switzerland, is closer kin to Gruyère than to Emmentaler, because it has smaller holes and a browner rind. Its flavor is quite sharp. *Jarlsberg*, Norway's Swiss, is made with skim milk. It has a smooth texture and a bland but pleasing flavor.

SHEEP'S & GOAT'S MILK CHEESES

Most fresh goat cheeses come from France—the label *chèvre* is your clue. There are a great many varieties. Among them are *Ste. Maure*—quite strong, creamy outside and chalky inside; *Montrachet*—medium-mild, log-shaped, sometimes rolled in charcoal which makes it saltier than the plain cheese; *crottin*—small and hard; *gèant* and *rondin*—small and very soft. All have the characteristic goat's-milk flavor you'll either love or hate. Many French goat cheeses are flavored with spices or herbs. Mild when young, they become exceedingly strong as they age.

Others in this category include Greek *feta*—white, salty and crumbly. Buy it by the piece or in a glass jar, packed in brine—the latter keeps better. *Gjetost* is Norwegian goat cheese with some cow's milk in it. A cooked cheese, its color and flavor are deliciously reminiscent of caramel.

Mild, almost bland *ricotta Romana*, a dried ricotta, is the only sheep cheese available outside of Italy for eating out of hand or grating. Fresh ricotta cheese is generally made locally from cows milk. Sheep cheeses don't travel well when fresh, so we seldom see them in the market. However, the harder *pecorino* or *kasseri*—it may be labeled *kashkavel*—are dry and can be shipped. You may also find domestic cheeses under these names, but most are made with cow's milk.

SEMISOFT CHEESES

Many are suitable for melting and cooking, as well as eating out of hand. Monterey Jack is sometimes classified with the semisoft cheeses rather than with the Cheddars because of its creamy texture. But many of the semisofts are much softer and creamier than Monterey Jack.

Doris McFerran Townsend

Doris McFerran Townsend is an untiring cook who can tell you nearly anything you want to know about food and cooking. She began majoring in Journalism in college, changed to Psychology and later branched out into cookbooks. For many years she was editor-in-chief of a New York publishing house that specialized in cookbooks. Her other experiences include food styling, recipe development and testing, demonstrating new food products and hosting a radio talk show. She has also written advertising copy, children's books and confession stories. Doris has authored over 20 cookbooks, including an encyclopedic volume on all aspects of food and cooking and cookbooks for various food corporations and appliance companies. Family, neighbors and friends anxiously await the testing of recipes for each new cookbook.

Doris and her husband, Bill, have developed their own advertising and publishing consulting business which they sandwich into a very active semi-retirement.

Pungent *Pont l'Evêque* has a golden-brown rind and is packaged in a flat square. *Fontina*—which is excellent for melting—can be either Italian or Scandinavian. Plain *mozzarella* is a good cooking cheese, but try the smoked variety for eating out of hand. Pear-shaped *provolone* is slightly ripened and lightly smoked. *Bonbel*, in a small, flattened round with a wax coating, has an intriguing, mildly tart taste. *Liederkranz*, when ripe—the only way its fans will eat it—has a very strong flavor and aroma. *Muenster* is mild if it's made in the United States, stronger if made elsewhere. Mild and soft *Bel Paese* is quickly recognized by the map of Italy or the Western hemisphere on its foil wrapper. *Port Salut* is soft and somewhat buttery with a distinctive flavor. *Havarti* is rather like Port Salut but firmer, and can be quite mild or very strong. *Cream Havarti* is softer, milder; *Tilsit* is the Scandinavian version of Havarti. *Beaufort* is a creamy semisoft goat cheese with a flavor, its fans claim, halfway between fontina and Gruyère. Bear in mind that all semisofts are reasonably mild when young, but most are very strong when well aged.

DUTCH CHEESES

Usually counted as a class by themselves, these are the nearest thing to the old down-on-the-farm cheese that was once a part of the diet of nearly everyone who had a cow. Cannonball-shaped *Edam*, made from skim milk, is covered with a red wax coating or a silver coating indicating a drier, stronger, longer-aged Edam. *Gouda*, made from whole milk, is smooth and mellow when young, and softer than Edam. *Leyden* is spiced with caraway seeds with a stronger flavor than the ones you use in cooking. *Roomkäse* is similar to Gouda, but richer because of a higher butterfat content. *Noekkelost* and *cuminost* are popular spiced Dutch cheeses.

SOFT-RIPENED CHEESES

Now we are coming to the more delicate cheeses, the ones most often served with crackers, fruit or wine. Not as delicate as double crèmes and triple crèmes, these are, nonetheless lovely and elegant. These creamy cheeses have a high butterfat content and a delicious off-white crust. *Brie* is the best-known. It has a silky texture and buttery color when it is *à point* or just right to eat. It comes in wheels ranging in size from small to enormous. French *V.C.N. Camembert* from Normandy, comes in small wheels only, has Brie's satiny texture but is more pungent when fully ripened. *Camembert* also comes in separately wrapped small wedges packaged in half-round boxes. *Coulommiers* is soft, mild and creamy, with a flavor reminiscent of both Brie and Camembert. Others you may want to sample are *tomme des neiges* and *Valembert*, both similar to Brie.

DOUBLE CRÈMES & TRIPLE CRÈMES

These are, indeed, the *crème de la crème* of the cheese world—rich, soft and buttery. Double crèmes have a 60 percent butterfat content, triple crèmes 70 to 75 percent. Some have a light edible crust like the soft-ripened cheeses—others are uncrusted. All are fresh or very lightly ripened. They should be eaten at room temperature while they are at their young best. Of the double crèmes, sample crusted *caprice des dieux*, *petit*

Suisse with a flavor like sweet sour cream, *suprême*, *Crèma Dania* and *fol amour*. Among the triple crèmes, browse until you find a favorite among *l'explorateur*, *Boursin*—which is flavored with herbs and garlic or peppered; *Boursault*—mild and airy; mild-flavored and creamy-textured *bellétoile* and *St. André*. Flavors differ somewhat from one another, but all are sinfully rich and unbelievably smooth.

This listing does not by any means embrace all the cheeses worth trying. I've not even touched on the blues—*Roquefort* from France is the queen, but don't overlook French *bleu de Bresse* and *belle Bressane*, Danish *Danablu*, British *Stilton* or Italy's great *Gorgonzola*. And don't forget to sample the grating cheeses such as *Asiago*, *Parmesan* and *Romano*.

Buying Cheese

Buying cheese at its peak of ripeness is a matter of know-how which comes with experience. But if you aren't sufficiently well versed, count on the cheese store expert to guide you. Doublecheck his expertise by sampling, because he may prefer cheese somewhat riper than suits your palate.

If you're buying a cheese that is new to you, buy only a small amount. Natural cheeses keep well. Cheddar, Swiss and hard-grating cheeses have the best keeping qualities, followed by Dutch cheeses and semisofts. All well-ripened cheeses have a reasonably long life. All cheeses, with the exception of process cheese, continue to ripen until the last crumb is eaten. In general, age brings sharper, more intensified flavor, an asset or liability depending on your taste buds. Fresh

and very mildly ripened cheeses do not age gracefully. They are best when soft and young. After a short time they spoil rather than ripen.

Parmesan and *Romano* are often pre-grated and packaged in jars or cardboard cartons. Romano has the somewhat sharper flavor of the two. However, the true flavor of either can't be experienced unless you buy a piece of cheese and use it freshly grated.

Be guided by your wants and needs, and by the kinds of cheese you purchase. Count on fresh cheeses lasting two weeks at the very longest. Some are much more perishable than others. The sturdier Cheddars and Swisses will still be usable—although considerably stronger in flavor—up to nine months if properly stored.

How Much To Buy

If a recipe calls for 2-1/2 cups of Cheddar cheese, how much do you buy? How about cottage cheese? If the recipe calls for 3 cups, will one carton be enough? Use this table when buying cheese for cooking.

Buy:	If you need:			
	cottage cheese	shredded	grated	crumbled
3/4 ounce			1/4 cup	
l ounce		1/4 cup	1/3 cup	1/4 cup
1-1/2 ounce			1/2 cup	
2 ounces	1/4 cup	1/2 cup	2/3 cup	1/2 cup
2-1/4 ounces			3/4 cup	
3 ounces		3/4 cup	1 cup	3/4 cup
4 ounces	1/2 cup	1 cup	1-1/3 cups	1 cup
8 ounces	1 cup	2 cups	2-2/3 cups	2 cups
12 ounces	1-1/2 cups	3 cups	4 cups	3 cups
1 pound	2 cups	4 cups		4 cups

Cheesemaking At Home

For many years cheesemaking was a home project throughout the world. Then specialization began to take place. The woman whose cheeses were creamier, better flavored and better textured than anyone else's went into the cheese business. Finally, cheese factories began to spring up. At last the time arrived when no one except remote farm families made cheese at home. New cheeses were developed and others were successfully or unsuccessfully copied across the world. Then came the day of the cheese shops.

We are still at that stage, but another movement is afoot.

Once again some of us are making cheese at home. Not the more complicated kinds, but good fresh pot or cottage cheese, cream cheese and some ripened ones, too.

Why do we do it? Because we enjoy it. Because making cheese at home is creative. And because the cheese we make is not only wonderfully good, but often more economical than its store-bought counterpart.

TOOLS YOU WILL NEED

- [ ] kettle, 6 quart or larger, see Guidelines, page 11
- [ ] bowls, 2-cup, 2-, 3- and 6-quart sizes
- [ ] pan, large flat, such as a dishpan
- [ ] spoons, long-handled wooden, plain and slotted
- [ ] spoons, plastic or stainless-steel measuring
- [ ] scales, kitchen or baby
- [ ] cups, 1-, 2- and 4-cup glass measuring
- [ ] thermometer, accurate deep-fat or candy, see Guidelines, page 11
- [ ] molds, small basket, pierced ceramic or glass as made for *coeur à la crème*
- [ ] cheesecloth or clean well-used muslin or linen cloth such as old sheets or napkins
- [ ] colander, large, enamel-coated, stainless-steel or plastic
- [ ] sieve, 2- or 3-cup, nylon or stainless-steel
- [ ] hoop, made from a 46-ounce juice can, see Guidelines, page 11

INGREDIENTS YOU WILL NEED

- [ ] milk, pasteurized homogenized or skim; Do not use evaporated, reconstituted dry, certified raw, or milk labeled *low fat*
- [ ] yogurt, whole-milk, unflavored
- [ ] buttermilk, cultured
- [ ] rennet tablets, household-strength, not dairy strength
- [ ] cream, heavy or whipping, half-and-half or light
- [ ] salt, not iodized

Guidelines For Home Cheesemakers

All utensils should be made of wood, stainless steel, nylon, plastic, glass, pottery, glass-ceramic or enamel-coated metal, but NEVER of uncoated aluminum, tin or cast iron. Metal objects, with the exception of stainless-steel, will impart an unpleasant flavor to cheese. Be certain all your equipment is scrupulously clean or unwanted bacteria may ruin your cheese.

Correct temperatures are critical in cheesemaking. To test your thermometer, attach it to the side of a pan and add water to cover the thermometer bulb. Bring the water to a boil. Thermometer should register 212°F (100°C). If thermometer registers 1° lower, add 1° to the temperature called for in the recipe when you cook the cheese. If the thermometer registers 1° higher, subtract 1° from the temperature called for in the recipe. If your thermometer is more than 5° high or low, get a new one.

When a recipe calls for cheesecloth, use the number of layers stated, or substitute a single or double layer of some old, often-laundered cotton or linen fabric such as bed sheets, unbleached muslin or large linen napkins. The cloth used can be laundered and reused.

If you want to make Homemade Swiss-Style Cheese you will need a *hoop*. You can make one from a 46-ounce juice can. First, punch 2 holes in top of the can with a can opener and empty the contents. Rinse the can but do not cut out top and bottom. Use a sharp nail and a hammer or a 1/16-inch drill bit to make about 10 vertical rows of holes around the side of the can. Leave a 1-1/2-inch space without holes around the bottom of the can. Punch or drill the holes 1 to 1-1/2 inches apart. Cut out and discard the punched top of the can. Place the can bottom-side down on a block of scrap wood. Working from the inside, use an ice pick to make 10 to 12 holes by striking the ice pick handle with a hammer. Smooth the rough edges around the holes on the inside of the can with a fine metal file. Wash the can thoroughly to remove any bits of metal.

Do you like the idea of making cheese? Roll up your sleeves and go to work. One note of caution: don't delve into great-grandmother's handwritten cookbook for recipes. Use my up-to-date ones, tailored for our present-day kitchens, equipment and ingredients. Keep everything clean, follow the recipes religiously and have fun!

Storing Cheese

Soft and fresh cheeses should be tightly covered and refrigerated. Store them in original containers or in containers with airtight covers.

Tightly wrap ripened cheeses in foil or plastic and store them in the coldest part of the refrigerator. Molding and drying out are the two enemies of cheese. Cheese in one piece keeps better than pre-sliced cheese. If you plan to store a cheese longer than a few days, butter the cut edge or seal it with paraffin to keep moisture in and air out. Cut mold off ripened cheese and feel perfectly safe in using the remainder. Store blue-veined cheeses in a covered glass dish that allows very little air to surround the cheese.

Strong cheeses pose a secondary storage problem. If not properly cared for, their odors are absorbed by delicately flavored foods such as butter. Wrap strong-flavored cheese tightly in plastic wrap and put into a container with an airtight cover.

Process cheeses and spreads can be stored on the shelf until opened, but must then be refrigerated. Protected well from air and moisture, process-cheese loaves and slices will keep well for several months. Flavored spreads will keep about three weeks if covered tightly.

Freeze cheese? That's an iffy question. When frozen, cheese looses both flavor and texture. By all means, freeze cheese rather than let it spoil, but use frozen cheese for cooking rather than for eating out of hand. Plan to keep frozen ripened cheese no more than six weeks, cream cheese up to eight weeks, and process cheese up to four months. The only cheese freezing really ruins is Neufchatel—its butterfat content is too low and its moisture content is too high.

GUIDE TO MANY POPULAR CHEESES

	Characteristics	Uses
American Pasteurized Process	Pale yellow to orange; smooth, semisoft to soft; mild Cheddar-like flavor; store several months	Blends well with other foods; use in sandwiches, sauces, dips, casseroles
Appenzeller (a-pent-SELL-er)	Deep cream to tan; somewhat crumbly; very strong flavor; ages slowly	Combine with other cheeses in raclette, casseroles, sauces
Asiago (ah-see-AH-goh)	Pale cream with a clear or brown wax cover; granular; strong to very strong	Grate into sauces; use as a garnish
beer cheese	See bierkäse	
Bel Paese (bel-pah-AY-say)	Pale cream; soft & buttery-smooth; mild to strong flavor	Serve with fruit, crackers; use in desserts, sauces, casseroles
bierkäse (BEER-khah-seh)	White with pale caramel colored edible crust; soft & creamy; sharp pungent flavor	Serve with crackers, beverages; use sparingly in sauces, other cooking
bleu (bluh)	See blue	
blue (bloo)	Pale with blue mold vein; crumbly; mild to sharp flavor grows stronger with age	Use sparingly in dressings, appetizers, dips, sauces, stuffings
bonbel (bon-BEL)	Pale cream; semisoft, buttery-smooth; mildly tart flavor grows stronger with age	Serve with fruit; use in sandwiches, salads
Boursault (boor-SOH)	White; smooth; mild; sometimes combined with herbs, spices, fruit or vegetables	Serve with fruit; use in desserts, dips, canapés
Boursin (boor-SAH)	White; creamy; flavored with garlic, herbs or pepper; similar to Boursault; short storage life	Spread on crackers; excellent on vegetables
brick (brik)	Deep yellow; smooth; mild to very strong flavor grows stronger with age	Serve with relishes; use in sandwiches, sauces, casseroles, baking
Brie (bree)	White with white to deep-brown edible crust; satin-smooth; mildly pungent; best when very soft but not runny; ages stronger and softer	Serve with fruit, wine, crackers or as an appetizer or spread
Caerphilly (car-FILL-ay)	White; crumbly Cheddar-like texture; creamy buttermilk flavor; melts readily	Serve on crackers or bread; use as a garnish; use in sauces, casseroles, salads
Camembert (KAM-ehm-beh)	Creamy colored with grayish edible crust; soft & creamy; very pungent when fully ripe	Serve with fruit, wine, crackers; or as an appetizer or spread
Chaource (chous)	White with chalky-white rind; smooth; delicately pungent flavor similar to Camembert	Serve with fruit, wine, crackers or as an appetizer or spread
Cheddar (CHEHD-er)	Naturally white, usually colored deep golden-yellow; dense but crumbly; mild, mellow, sharp & extra-sharp	Serve with fruit, crackers, relishes; use in sandwiches, sauces, casseroles, baking
Cheshire (CHEHSH-er)	Deep golden yellow; smooth, crumbly; early, medium & late flavors are mild to sharp	Serve with fruit, crackers, relishes; use in sandwiches, sauces, casseroles
chèvre Valençay (shehvr-vah-lehn-SAY)	French goat cheese; flat-topped pyramid; pale ash color with powdery edible crust; salty, tart	Serve with fruit, crackers, relishes; use in sauces, casseroles
Colby (COHL-bee)	Golden-yellow; open, somewhat granular; mild Cheddar flavor grows stronger with age	Serve with fruit, crackers, relishes; use in sandwiches, sauces, casseroles, baking
cottage (COT-tage)	Large or small soft curds, creamed or uncreamed; mild; sometimes called *pot cheese*	Serve as is or mix with vegetables, fruit, meat; use in baking, casseroles
cream (creem)	White; soft; mild flavor; short storage life	Use in desserts, sauces; combine with spices for dips, spreads
Crèma Dania (KREHM-ah-DAWN-yah)	White with a thin waxy rind; delicate, smooth; slightly sweet; ages slowly; similar to Brie	Serve with fruit or wine; use as an appetizer or spread

doux de montagne *(doo-duh-mohn-TAHN-yah)*	Pale with a tough russet rind; smooth, crumbly; tangy flavor, mildly sour aftertaste	Use in baking, sauces, casseroles
Edam *(EE-dam)*	Cream with red or silver wax cover; semisoft to firm; milky nut-like flavor; mild to strong	Serve as a snack; use in sandwiches, sauces, casseroles
Emmental *(EM-en-tall)*	See Emmentaler	
Emmentaler *(EM-en-tall-er)*	Original Swiss cheese; white; smooth with large holes; medium to sharp nut-like flavor	Serve with fruit desserts; use in sandwiches, sauces, casseroles
Esrom *(EHZ-ruhm)*	Cream color; semisoft; strong, very distinctive flavor	Serve with fruit or vegetables; use sparingly in sauces, casseroles
feta *(FEHT-ah)*	White; crumbly & grainy; strong salty pickle-like flavor; sometimes packed in brine; cooking cheese of Greece	Use in salads, sauces, casseroles
fontina *(fon-TEE-nah)*	Pale yellow; smooth & semisoft, sometimes has small holes; delicate sweet nut-like flavor	Serve with fruit or crackers; use in sandwiches, sauces, casseroles
gjetost *(YET-ohst)*	Caramel color and flavor; smooth rather firm; chewy, candy-like	Use in sauces, casseroles; serve with crackers; shred into egg dishes
Gorgonzola *(gor-gon-ZOH-lah)*	Italian blue-veined cheese; soft & crumbly; very strong flavor	Use sparingly in salads, dressings, sauces, dips, appetizers
Gouda *(GOO-dah)*	Pale with red or pale-gold wax cover; smooth, semisoft to hard; milky nut-like flavor grows stronger with age; higher fat content than Edam	Serve as a snack; use in sandwiches, sauces, casseroles
Gruyère *(groo-YEHR)*	Cream color; smooth-textured Swiss with small holes; medium-sharp	Serve with fruit or relishes; use in sandwiches, sauces, salads, casseroles
Herkimer *(HUR-kah-mer)*	New York Cheddar; very pale yellow; smooth; sharp to very sharp flavor; drier than most Cheddars	Serve with fruits or relishes; use in sandwiches, sauces, casseroles
Hervè *(her-VAY)*	Looks and tastes like Limburger; white; soft, buttery-smooth; very strong; softens with age	Serve on black bread or thick crackers
jack *(jak)*	See Monterey Jack	
Jarlsberg *(YARLS-berg)*	Norwegian Swiss; creamy white; smooth with small holes; mild somewhat bland flavor	Serve with fruit, relishes; use in sandwiches, fresh or jellied salads, sauces, casseroles
Leyden *(LAY-den)*	Pale yellow-orange; smooth; spiced with strong-flavored caraway seeds	Use in dark bread sandwiches, salads; shred over sauerkraut
Liederkranz *(LEE-der-krants)*	Similar to Brie or Camembert; very strong flavor & aroma; short storage life	Serve with fruit, wine, crackers; use in sandwiches, dressings
Limburger *(LIM-ber-ger)*	White with red-yellow rind; soft, buttery-smooth; extremely strong flavor	Serve on black bread or thick crackers
Longhorn *(LONG-horn)*	Golden-yellow; open, granular & crumbly; mild Cheddar flavor; similar to Colby	Serve as a snack; use in sandwiches, sauces, casseroles
mascarpone *(mas-kar-POHN-ah)*	Similar to ricotta; buttery & granular; slightly acid flavor; short storage life	Serve with fruit & vegetables; use in dips, spreads
Monterey Jack *(MONT-er-ay-JAK)*	Creamy white; smooth, semisoft to soft; mild flavor	Serve as a snack; use in sauces, sandwiches, casseroles
mozzarella *(mohd-sah-REHL-lah)*	Creamy white; semisoft to soft smooth texture is rubbery when cold; very mild flavor; short storage life; similar to scamorze	Use in sauces, casseroles, fillings, sandwiches
Muenster *(MUHN-ster)*	Creamy white; smooth, somewhat rubbery; mild to strong flavor; similar to fontina	Serve with fruit, as a snack; use in cooking, sauces, casseroles, sandwiches
Müenster *(MUHN-ster)*	See Muenster	

Neuchâtel *(NUH-shaw-tell)*	Cream cheese of Switzerland; see Neufchatel	
Neufchâtel *(NUH-shaw-tell)*	French cream cheese; soft, smooth, creamy; mildly acid flavor; short storage life	Use in desserts, dips, sauces, spreads
noekkelost *(NOHK-ehl-ohst)*	Pale yellow-orange; semisoft, smooth; usually flavored with cloves, caraway or cumin; similar to Leyden	Use in dark bread sandwiches, salads; shred over sauerkraut
Parmesan *(PAR-mah-zahn)*	Pale yellow; granular hard-grating cheese; sharp flavor	Use as a garnish on casseroles, soups; use in salads, sauces
Pont l'Evêque *(pohn-lay-VEHK)*	Pale yellow with golden-brown rind; soft creamy; sharp flavor similar to Camembert	Serve with fruit or wine; use as an appetizer or spread
Port du Salut *(pohr-doo-sah-LOO)*	See Port Salut	
Port Salut *(pohr-sah-LOO)*	Pale yellow with brownish edible crust; soft, buttery texture similar to cream cheese; strong distinctive flavor	Serve with fruit, vegetables; use in sandwiches or on eggs
primost *(PREE-most)*	Pale cream with pale-brown edible crust; semisoft; mild tart-sweet buttermilk flavor	Serve with crackers, fruit, vegetables; use in sauces, casseroles, spreads, baking
provolone *(proh-voh-LOH-nee)*	Creamy white; pear-shaped; very firm; pleasantly sharp, lightly smoked flavor	Use in Italian cooking, sauces, appetizers, canapés, antipasto
raclette *(rack-LET)*	Pale-cream Swiss; smooth, somewhat rubbery; mild to sharp flavor; similar to Emmentaler	Melt to use with vegetables as in raclette recipes
ricotta *(rih-KOT-ah)*	Very small white curds; soft & grainy but smoother than cottage cheese; mild	Use in desserts, casseroles, sauces, vegetable stuffings
Romano *(roh-MAH-noh)*	Pale yellow; grainy hard-grating cheese, very sharp flavor	Use as a garnish on soups, casseroles; use in salads, sauces
Roquefort *(ROHK-for)*	Blue-veined cheese; semisoft; very sharp peppery flavor; ages slowly	Use sparingly in dressings, dips, sauces, stuffings, fruit desserts
samsø *(sam-soh)*	Danish Swiss; creamy white; firm & smooth with round holes; mild, sweet nut-like flavor	Use in sandwiches, sauces, casseroles, salads
sapsago *(sap-SAY-goh)*	Light-green color & distinctive pleasing flavor come from clover leaves; hard-grating cheese	Use in salads, egg dishes, to garnish cream soups
scamorze *(skah-MORD-zee)*	Pale yellow; pear-shaped; smooth & rubbery; mild flavor; similar to mozzarella	Serve as a snack with crackers, relishes; use in sandwiches, sauces, casseroles, vegetable & meat stuffings
Stilton *(STILL-ton)*	King of blue-veined cheeses; dense but crumbly; very sharp, rich flavor; melts like Cheddar	Serve with dessert wines; use in sandwiches, sauces, casseroles
St. Marcellin *(sah-MAR-se-lah)*	Goat cream cheese; often wrapped in chestnut leaves; white; crumbly; mild, slightly salty	Best eaten fresh; serve as a snack with crackers; use in sandwiches, sauces
Swiss	Creamy white; smooth, almost rubbery texture with large holes; mild to sharp distinctive nut-like flavor; also see Emmentaler, Gruyere, Jarlsberg, Tillamook, samsø	Serve with fruit, fruit desserts, relishes; use in sandwiches, sauces, salads, casseroles
teleme *(TELL-eh-mee)*	White; soft elastic texture similar to feta; sharp distinctive pickle-like flavor	Use in salads, sauces, casseroles
Tillamook *(TILL-ah-mook)*	Oregon Cheddar; bright yellow; smooth & firm; mild to sharp flavor	Serve with fruit, relishes; use in sandwiches, sauces, salads, casseroles
Tilsit *(TIHL-siht)*	Pale yellow; medium-firm texture sometimes has small round holes; mild to strong flavor; sometimes flavored with caraway seeds	Use in egg dishes; use mild flavored Tilsit in sandwiches, sauces, casseroles
tybo *(tie-boh)*	Cream-colored with non-edible red wax cover; firm & smooth; mild flavor; similar to samsø	Use in sandwiches, sauces, casseroles, salads
Wensleydale *(WEHNS-slee-dale)*	White with blue veins; smooth somewhat crumbly; rich, slightly sour flavor; similar to Stilton	Serve with dessert wines; use in sandwiches, sauces, casseroles

Homemade Cheese

You won't be able to buy the cheeses found in this section in your supermarket. They are truly homemade cheeses.

Cheesemaking isn't difficult, but once you start, there's no turning back. Before embarking on a cheesemaking project, read the recipe all the way through and make certain you understand it completely. Then assemble all the necessary equipment and ingredients. You'll need a *colander* or a large *sieve* for most of the recipes in this section. A colander is a large, bowl-shaped container perforated with 1/8-inch to 1/16-inch holes. Sieves are made of open mesh attached to a frame with a long handle. In most of the recipes, I've called for a colander so both your hands will be free to handle the cheese mixture. Whichever you choose, be sure it is made of nylon, plastic, stainless-steel or enamel-coated metal. Other materials may cause your cheese to change color and develop a metallic taste.

Use household-strength *rennet tablets*, not commercial strength. They are available at most supermarkets, drugstores and dairy supply stores. If you have difficulty locating rennet tablets, look for *Junket tablets*. **Do not use Junket powder**. It is a completely different product flavored for making puddings.

Begin your cheesemaking experience with Labna, a simple cheese made from yogurt. It is similar to whole-milk *ricotta* cheese in flavor and texture and may be substituted for ricotta in recipes such as lasagna and Slimmer's Delight, page 143. Serve Labna with fruit, crumble it into a salad or process it in the blender and use it as the base for a sandwich spread.

Two homemade cheeses, Farm-Style Buttermilk Cheese and Rich Cream-Style Cheese are similar to *cream* cheese. They can be used in place of commercial cream cheese in most recipes. Farm-Style Buttermilk Cheese offers some special bonuses. Although it resembles cream cheese, it has half the calories, twice the protein and a third of the fat. Use it in Farm-Style Buttermilk Cheesecake, page 146, for fewer calories.

Easter Sunday Breakfast
Mint-Garnished Fresh Pineapple
Pork Sausages
Cerek, page 19
Polka Dot Quick Bread, page 121

Pennsylvania Dutch Pot Cheese

Store the cheese inside a kitchen cupboard while it ripens.

Country-Style Cottage Cheese, page 17

2 tablespoons butter, room temperature

2 tablespoons heavy cream or whipping cream

1/2 teaspoon dried sage leaves, crumbled

1 tablespoon minced onion

Salt and pepper to taste

Prepare Country-Style Cottage Cheese. Place in a stone crock or glass jar. Cover with a tight-fitting lid or plastic wrap. Let ripen to desired sharpness, 4 to 8 days. Store 4 days at 75°F (25°C), 6 days at 72°F (22°C) or 8 days at 65°F (20°C). Place crock or jar in a large pot. Pour hot water 4 inches deep into pot. Stirring cheese constantly, heat slowly until cheese is melted and smooth. Stir in butter, cream, sage, onion and salt and pepper to taste. Spoon cheese into three 1-cup jars with tight-fitting lids. Cover and refrigerate. Use within 2 weeks. Makes 3 cups.

Rich Cream-Style Cheese

Add three tablespoons of your favorite chopped fresh herb for Herbed Cream-Style Cheese.

1 qt. half-and-half or light cream

1/2 pt. heavy cream or whipping cream

2 tablespoons cultured buttermilk

Salt to taste

Combine half-and-half or light cream and heavy cream or whipping cream in a medium-heavy sauce-pan. Attach a candy or deep-fat thermometer to the side of the saucepan. Heat cream mixture to 90°F (30°C) over low heat. Stir in buttermilk. Pour cream mixture into a large bowl; cover with plastic wrap. Enclose entire bowl in a large bath towel or blanket. Place in a warm area 24 to 48 hours until mixture develops the consistency of soft yogurt. Mixture will not flow when bowl is slowly tipped from side to side. Cut 3 pieces of cheesecloth large enough to line a large colander and extend 3 inches over edge. Rinse in cold water. Wring out excess water; line colander. Place colander in sink. Slowly pour cooked cream mixture into colander. Let drain 15 minutes. Place colander in a deep bowl. Cover with plastic wrap to make an airtight seal over colander and bowl. Refrigerate 12 to 18 hours until well drained. Cut 12 pieces of cheesecloth 8 inches square. Rinse in cold water. Wring out excess water. Make 3 stacks of 4 pieces each. Spoon cream mixture into a clean bowl. Salt lightly to taste. Divide into 3 portions. Wrap each portion in 4 pieces of wet cheesecloth. Tie securely. Press each cheesecloth-wrapped portion into a 1-cup coeur à la crème mold or small strainer or shape into a round ball. Place a rack in a shallow pan. Place molds, strainers or balls of cheese on rack. Cover pan and cheese with plastic wrap to make an airtight seal. Refrigerate 36 to 48 hours until firm. Remove from molds. Unwrap to serve or cover and store in refrigerator. Use within 5 days. Makes about 2-1/2 cups.

Sour milk can sometimes be substituted for buttermilk in a recipe, but never in a homemade cheese recipe.

Country-Style Cottage Cheese

Serve plain or creamed to discover the taste of real *cottage cheese.*

4 qts. skim milk
1/2 rennet tablet
1/4 cup cold water

1/4 cup cultured buttermilk
Salt to taste
Ice water

Pour skim milk into a 6-quart double boiler. Pour water 2 to 3 inches deep in outer pot. Bring to a simmer over medium heat. Attach a candy or deep-fat thermometer to side of inner pot. Heat milk to 72°F (22°C). Dissolve rennet in 1/4 cup cold water. Stir rennet mixture and buttermilk into heated skim milk, blending thoroughly. Cover and remove from heat. Let stand in a warm place (72° to 80°F, 22° to 25°C) 12 to 18 hours until a firm curd forms. To maintain this temperature, replace hot water in outer pot as needed or place top of double boiler in an unheated oven with pilot light or interior light bulb burning. When curd has reached consistency of a fairly firm pudding, slowly insert a long thin stainless-steel knife into cheese on side of pot opposite you. Draw knife through cheese toward you. Carefully remove knife and repeat cutting at 1/2-inch intervals. Turn pot 1/4 turn; repeat cutting at 1/2-inch intervals. Insert knife again in the same cuts, but on a diagonal. Cut curds on diagonal. Turn pot 1/4 turn and repeat cutting on diagonal. Place pot containing cut curds over hot water. Bring water to just below boiling. Heat until curds reach 110°F (45°C). Keep curds at this temperature 18 minutes, stirring gently every 5 minutes. While curds heat, cut 4 pieces of cheesecloth large enough to line a large colander and extend 3 inches over edge. Rinse in cold water. Wring out excess water; line colander. Place colander in sink. Pour curds and whey into colander; let drain 8 to 10 minutes. Fill a large pot with ice water. Gather cheesecloth together at top. Lift from colander and immerse in ice water. Gently press bag and curds. Dip bag of curds in and out of ice water until rinsed and chilled. Lift from water and gently squeeze out excess liquid. Return to colander and let drain 1-1/2 to 2 hours until liquid no longer drips from cheese. Place cheese in a clean medium bowl, scraping curds from cheesecloth. Stir in salt to taste. Refrigerate in an airtight container. Use within 4 to 5 days. Makes about 3 cups.

Variation

Creamed cottage cheese: Stir in 1/3 cup heavy cream or whipping cream.

Labna

This simple yogurt cheese is a good first project. Use it in place of ricotta cheese.

1 pint unflavored whole-milk yogurt

Cut 2 pieces of cheesecloth large enough to line a 6-inch sieve or strainer and extend 3 inches over the edge. Rinse in cold water. Wring out excess water; line sieve or strainer. Place over a bowl and pour in yogurt. Let stand 30 minutes; discard drippings. Gather corners of cheesecloth together and tie with string to make a bag. Hang the bag from a faucet or hook. Place a bowl under bag to catch drippings. Let drain about 12 hours until cheese is firm. Discard drippings. Untie bag and place cheese in a small bowl with a tight cover. Refrigerate and use within 2 weeks. Makes 1 cup.

Farm-Style Buttermilk Cheese

Perfect to use in Cheese Blintzes, page 27, or Farm-Style Buttermilk Cheesecake, page 146.

4 qts. whole milk
1 qt. cultured buttermilk

1 teaspoon salt

Combine milk and buttermilk in a 6- to 8-quart heavy pot or Dutch oven. Fasten a candy or deep-fat thermometer to the side of the pot. Heat slowly over medium-low heat. Stir slowly and gently every 7 to 8 minutes to prevent scorching. Too-frequent stirring breaks up curds. Heat mixture to 170° to 175°F (75° to 80°C). Hold at this temperature 45 to 70 minutes. If temperature rises above 175°F (80°C), remove pot from heat until temperature lowers. While mixture cooks, cut 3 pieces of cheesecloth large enough to line a large colander and extend 3 inches over edge. Rinse in cold water. Wring out excess water; line colander. Place colander in a large bowl. Milk mixture will separate into thick white *curds* and a thin watery liquid called *whey*. Use a slotted spoon to place curds in lined colander. When most of the curds have been transferred, place colander in sink and slowly pour in remaining curds and whey. Discard whey. Let curds drain 2 to 3 hours. Turn cheese into a medium bowl, scraping curds from cheesecloth. Stir in salt with a fork. Refrigerate and use within 1 week. Makes about 4 cups or 2 pounds.

How to Make
Farm-Style Buttermilk Cheese

1/Cut 3 layers of cheesecloth large enough to line a large colander and extend 3 inches over edge.

2/Let curds drain 2 to 3 hours, then turn into a clean bowl, scraping curds from cheesecloth.

Cerek

Traditionally served on Easter morning, this Slavic cheese will make any morning seem special.

12 eggs
2 cups whole milk
2 cups water
1 teaspoon butter, softened

1/8 teaspoon salt
1/2 cup sugar
1 egg yolk
2 tablespoons whole milk

Break 12 eggs into a shallow 2-quart glass or enameled saucepan. Stir with a fork to combine whites and yolks. Stir in 2 cups milk, water, butter, salt and sugar. Bring to a simmer over low heat. Stirring constantly, simmer about 15 minutes until curds form. Cut 3 pieces of cheesecloth large enough to line a large colander and extend 3 inches over edge. Rinse in cold water. Wring out excess water; line colander. Place colander in a large bowl. Pour egg mixture into colander. Gather top of cheesecloth and tie with string to make a bag. Hang bag from a faucet or hook. Let drain over a bowl about 30 minutes until a ball of cheese forms. Discard drippings. Preheat oven to 375°F (190°C). Lightly butter a shallow 9-inch square baking dish. In a small bowl, use a fork to beat egg yolk and 2 tablespoons milk. Place cheese ball in prepared baking dish. Brush with milk mixture. Bake 10 to 12 minutes in preheated oven until very lightly browned. Makes about 1 pound.

Potato Cheese

Sour milk by adding 1 tablespoon white vinegar or lemon juice to 1 cup of sweet milk.

2 qts. water
5 lbs. potatoes
2 tablespoons white vinegar

About 2 cups milk
Salt to taste

Bring water to a boil in an 8- to 10-quart saucepan. Cook potatoes in boiling water until tender when pierced with a fork. Pour vinegar into a 2-cup measure. Add milk to make 2 cups. Let stand 15 minutes. Peel and mash potatoes until no lumps remain. Stir in soured milk and salt to taste. Turn out onto a large flat surface. Knead about 8 minutes. Cover and let stand 3 days in a cool area. Place 6 to 12 small baskets or pierced molds on racks. Knead potato mixture again 8 minutes. Pack into baskets or molds. Place racks with baskets or molds in a cool area. Lightly cover; let cheese dry 3 days. Pack baskets or molds into large stone crocks, separating with waxed paper or plastic wrap. Let stand in a cool place 14 days or longer. Flavor develops with age. Cheese will store several months in the refrigerator. Makes 6 to 12 cheeses.

Columbians enjoy a hot chocolate drink into which they drop cubes of mild-flavored homemade cheese.

Homemade Swiss-Style Cheese

Curing or aging at a cool temperature takes longer but gives a finer texture and flavor.

5-1/2 qts. whole milk	2 tablespoons salt
2 teaspoons plain yogurt	1 qt. cool water
1 rennet tablet	Salt
1/2 cup cool water	Water

Combine milk and yogurt in a 6-quart pot. Stir well. Let stand at room temperature 25 minutes. Remove 4 cups milk mixture to a medium bowl; set aside. Attach a candy or deep-fat thermometer to side of pot. Stirring constantly with a large wooden fork or slotted wooden spoon, heat to 110°F (45°C). Stir in remaining milk mixture. Cool to 90°F (30°C). Remove from heat. Crush rennet tablet between 2 spoons. Dissolve in 1/2 cup cool water. Stir into milk mixture. Let mixture stand at room temperature 20 to 25 minutes until consistency of soft custard. Slowly insert a long thin stainless-steel knife into cheese on side of pot opposite you. Draw knife through cheese toward you. Carefully remove knife and repeat cutting at 1/2-inch intervals. Turn pot 1/4 turn. Repeat cutting at 1/2-inch intervals. Let stand 5 minutes. Use a wooden fork or spoon to stir mixture slowly in a figure-8 pattern for 3 minutes. Let rest 3 minutes. Repeat stirring and resting process 2 more times. Curds will be fairly firm and about the size of kernels of corn. Stirring constantly, heat mixture to 88° to 90°F (30° to 32°C), 3 to 5 minutes. Do not let mixture exceed 90°F (32°C). Remove from heat and continue to stir in a circular motion 8 minutes. Place a rack over a large bowl. Place a cheese hoop in sink or in a deep pot. Use a skimming ladle or slotted spoon to transfer curds from cooking pot to hoop. Flatten surface of cheese with back of spoon. After most of whey has drained off, place hoop on rack over bowl. Let curds stand in hoop 24 hours at 72°F (22°C). After about 6 hours, remove cheese from hoop, turn over and return to hoop. Repeat process 2 more times during 24 hours. In a large bowl, dissolve 2 tablespoons salt in 1 quart cool water. Remove cheese from hoop and place in salt solution. Soak 3 hours, turning after 1-1/2 hours. Wash rack; place over a glass or plastic bowl 2/3 full of water. Remove cheese from brine and place on rack over bowl. Invert a second glass or plastic bowl to cover cheese. Keep cheese at 55°F (15°C) 3 days. To cure cheese, turn wheel of cheese once each day for 3 to 5 weeks. Each time cheese is turned, wash and dry rack. When cheese is turned, blot surface very gently with a clean cloth wrung out in a fresh salt-water solution, using 1-1/2 teaspoons salt and 1 cup water. Do not rub cheese. A soft white rind and then a pink rind will develop during curing process. Makes one 1-pound wheel.

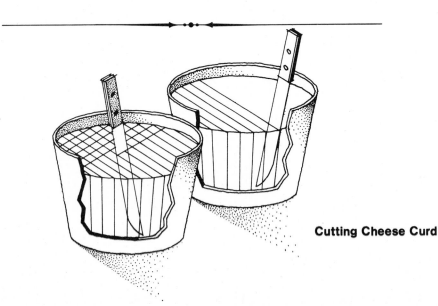

Cutting Cheese Curd

1/Use a long, thin knife to cut cheese at 1/2 inch intervals. Turn pan and continue cutting.

2/Use a skimming ladle or slotted spoon to tranfer curds from pot to hoop.

How to Make
Homemade Swiss-Style Cheese

3/Remove cheese from brine and place on a rack over bowl of water. Cover with another bowl.

4/Each time cheese is turned, blot it lightly with a cloth dipped in a fresh salt-water solution.

Breakfast

A good breakfast gives you energy for the day's activities. Because cheese is rich in protein, it's an excellent breakfast food and can satisfy most appetites until time for lunch. For the weight-conscious, whole-wheat toast topped with *ricotta* cheese and slices of fresh fruit is a filling and nutritious breakfast. If calories are not a problem for you, enjoy Fruited Cottage Pancakes—hearty breakfast fare with sieved *cottage* cheese and sour cream in the batter—and top them with a special hot raspberry sauce.

Because cheese is made from milk, it contains most of the nutrients found in milk, including protein, calcium, vitamin A, riboflavin, zinc and traces of other elements. The nutrient content of a particular cheese depends on how it is processed. It takes about ten pounds of milk to make one pound of cheese. Cheeses made from curds formed by rennet or bacteria, such as *Cheddars* or *Dutch* cheeses, retain about 80% of the calcium content of milk. Acid-formed curds, such as *cottage* cheese and *Neufchâtel*, retain only about 20% of the calcium. Cheeses made from whole milk are good sources of vitamin A and riboflavin because these nutrients are held in the butterfat.

Eggs and cheese blend well in omelets and in various baked and scrambled-egg dishes. Double-Delight Omelet is prepared by the French omelet method. Pour the egg mixture into a medium-hot omelet pan or skillet containing melted butter or margarine. While stirring with the back of a fork held flat on the bottom of the pan, slide the pan briskly back and forth over the heat until the omelet is almost set on the bottom and slightly soft on top. The top will continue cooking after you remove the pan from the heat. Spoon the filling onto the middle of the omelet, fold the sides over the filling and slide the omelet onto a platter.

You'll discover more dishes in this section you'll want to try—delightful breakfast breads, tasty but quick-and-easy dishes for hurry-up mornings and brunch dishes to please everyone.

Before-the-Game Brunch
Half & Half Orange & Cranberry Juice
Broiled Canadian Bacon
Cheddar Baked Toast, page 24
Cinnamon Sprinkled Apple Slices
Company Brunch Babkas, page 124

Big Dutch Boy

This baked batter is similar to Yorkshire pudding.

4 slices bacon, cut in 1/4-inch pieces
1 cup all-purpose flour
1 tablespoon sugar
3/4 teaspoon salt
3 eggs

2 cups milk
1-1/2 to 2 cups halved strawberries, orange
    chunks, poached apple chunks, whole-
    berry cranberry sauce or pineapple chunks
2 cups shredded Edam cheese (8 oz.)

Preheat oven to 375°F (190°C). In a heavy 10-inch skillet with ovenproof handle, cook bacon over medium heat until crisp. Reserve about 4 tablespoons bacon drippings in skillet; set aside. Sift flour, sugar and salt into a medium bowl; set aside. Beat eggs in a small bowl. Stir in milk. Beat egg mixture into flour mixture until batter is smooth. Heat reserved bacon drippings over medium-high heat. Pour batter into hot bacon drippings. Bake about 30 minutes in preheated oven until golden brown and puffed at edge. Remove from oven; let stand 5 minutes. Center will sink. Top with fruit; sprinkle with cheese. Bake again until cheese is very soft, about 5 minutes. Makes 4 to 6 servings.

Little Cheddar Biscuits

Split and toasted, the leftover biscuits are almost better than the first time around!

2 cups all-purpose flour
1 teaspoon dry mustard
1 teaspoon paprika
1/4 teaspoon baking powder

1 cup butter or margarine, room temperature
2 cups shredded sharp Cheddar cheese (8 oz.)
1 teaspoon Worcestershire sauce

Combine flour, dry mustard, paprika and baking powder in a medium bowl. Set aside. Beat butter or margarine in a large bowl by hand or with an electric mixer on medium speed until fluffy. Slowly beat in cheese and Worcestershire sauce. Gradually add flour mixture, stirring with a fork until combined. On a lightly floured surface, shape dough into a long roll about 1-3/4 inches in diameter. Wrap in plastic wrap or foil. Place on a platter. Refrigerate 2 hours or overnight. Preheat oven to 325°F (165°C). Slice dough about 1/3-inch thick. With hands, roll each slice into a ball. Flatten slightly. Place on an ungreased baking sheet about 2 inches apart. Bake 8 minutes in preheated oven. Biscuits will only brown slightly on bottom. Makes about 36 biscuits.

Variations

Biscuits may be made larger. Cut slices about 2/3-inch thick. Roll into balls. Flatten each ball to about 2 inches in diameter. Bake 10 minutes.

Hunt Breakfast Biscuits: Cream 1/2 cup butter or margarine, 1/2 teaspoon dry mustard and 1/2 teaspoon onion juice. Split and toast cooked biscuits. Spread with butter or margarine mixture. Place thin slices of country-style ham between biscuit halves. Serve immediately.

Fruited Cottage Pancakes

Spiced fruit sauce is a delicious change from syrup as a topper for pancakes.

Fruit Sauce, see below
1 cup small-curd cottage cheese (8 oz.)
1 cup dairy sour cream
4 eggs

1 cup all-purpose flour
2 tablespoons sugar
1/2 teaspoon salt
1/4 cup butter or margarine, melted

Fruit Sauce:
2 (8-oz.) pkgs. frozen raspberries, thawed
1 tablespoon cornstarch

1/2 teaspoon lemon juice

Prepare Fruit Sauce. With the back of a spoon, force cottage cheese through a sieve into a medium bowl. Stir in sour cream. Add eggs one at a time, beating well after each addition. Combine flour, sugar and salt in a sifter. Sift into cheese mixture all at once, beating to blend well. Let batter stand at room temperature 10 minutes. Preheat griddle according to manufacturer's instructions or until a drop of water bounces across surface. Brush with melted butter or margarine. Stir pancake batter. Use 1/4 cup batter for each pancake. Pour onto preheated griddle, 1 inch apart. Bake 2 to 3 minutes on each side until golden brown. Add butter or margarine to griddle as needed. Keep cooked pancakes warm. Serve in stacks of 3 pancakes with warm fruit sauce. Makes about 15 pancakes.

Fruit Sauce:
Drain juice from raspberries into a small saucepan. Stir in cornstarch until dissolved. Bring to a boil over medium heat until thickened, stirring continually. Remove from heat and stir in lemon juice; fold in drained raspberries. Keep warm. Makes about 2 cups.

Fruit Sauce Variation
Coarsely chop 2 (8-ounce) packages mixed dried fruit. In a medium saucepan, combine chopped dried fruit, 2/3 cup sugar, 6 whole cloves, 3 (1-inch) pieces stick cinnamon and 1/4 teaspoon nutmeg. Pour water 1 inch deep into saucepan. Stir to blend. Bring to a boil over medium heat. Cover and reduce heat. Simmer 30 to 35 minutes until fruit is tender. Stir in 1/4 teaspoon vanilla extract. Refrigerate 30 minutes to blend flavors. Reheat to serve. Makes about 2 cups.

Baked Cheddar Toast

Serve with tart currant jelly or spiced applesauce.

1 cup heavy cream or whipping cream
1 cup shredded Cheddar cheese (4 oz.)
1/4 teaspoon white pepper

1/2 teaspoon ground nutmeg
4 eggs, well beaten
12 slices bread

In the top of a double boiler, combine cream, cheese, white pepper and nutmeg. Stir over hot water until cheese melts and mixture is blended. Cool to lukewarm. Generously butter a large baking sheet; set aside. Preheat oven to 375°F (190°C). Beat eggs into cooled cheese mixture. Cut bread slices diagonally. Dip bread pieces into cheese mixture 1 at a time. Place 1/2 inch apart on prepared baking sheet. Bake until browned and bubbly, about 15 minutes. Makes 6 servings.

Creamy Orange Loaf

Pans are floured to help with the browning process.

2-1/4 cups all-purpose flour
1 tablespoon baking powder
1 teaspoon salt
3/4 cup milk
1/4 cup water
1/2 cup butter or margarine,
   room temperature

1-1/4 cups sugar
2 eggs
1 (8-oz.) pkg. cream cheese,
   cut in 1/2-inch cubes
1/2 cup chopped walnuts
2 tablespoons grated orange peel
2 tablespoons sugar

Preheat oven to 375°F (190°C). Grease and lightly flour a 9" x 5" loaf pan; set aside. Sift flour, baking powder and salt onto a 12-inch square of waxed paper; set aside. Combine milk and water; set aside. In a medium bowl, cream butter or margarine and 1-1/4 cups sugar with electric mixer on medium speed. Beat in eggs. By hand, stir in flour mixture and milk mixture alternately, blending after each addition. Fold in cream cheese cubes, nuts and 1 tablespoon orange peel. Spoon into prepared loaf pan. In a small bowl, blend remaining 1 tablespoon orange peel and 2 tablespoons sugar. Sprinkle over loaf. Press lightly into surface. Bake about 1 hour 15 minutes in preheated oven. Cool on a rack 10 minutes. Remove from pan and cool on rack 20 minutes longer. Makes 1 loaf.

Gjetost & Jelly Omelet

Never use grape jelly in jelly omelets. It stains the omelet an unappetizing blue-brown.

4 eggs, separated
1/4 cup water
1/4 teaspoon salt
1/4 teaspoon cream of tartar
1 tablespoon butter or margarine

1/2 cup currant or other tart jelly
3/4 cup shredded gjetost cheese (3 oz.)
1 tablespoon butter or margarine,
   room temperature

Combine egg whites, water, salt and cream of tartar in a large bowl. Beat with electric mixer on high speed until stiff but not dry. Without washing beaters, beat egg yolks in a small bowl until thickened and pale. Fold beaten egg yolks into beaten egg whites. Preheat oven to 325°F (165°C). Over medium heat, melt 1 tablespoon butter or margarine in a 10-inch omelet pan or skillet with ovenproof handle. Pour in egg mixture. Lower heat and cook until top is puffed and bottom is set. Do not stir. Place omelet and pan into preheated oven. Bake until a knife inserted in center comes out dry, about 10 minutes. Break up jelly with a fork; set aside. In a small bowl, combine 1/2 cup of the cheese and 1 tablespoon room temperature butter or margarine. Remove omelet from oven. Turn oven control to broil. Loosen edges of omelet with the blade of a knife. Slide omelet onto an ovenproof platter. Score center with dull side of a knife. Place jelly on one half of omelet; fold other half over jelly. Top with butter-cheese mixture. Sprinkle with remaining cheese. Broil until cheese melts, about 3 minutes. Makes 3 servings.

Cheese Blintzes

You can change the topping to hot cherry or apple pie filling and a dollop of sour cream.

Cheese Filling, see below
3/4 cup all-purpose flour
1/2 teaspoon salt
1 cup milk

2 eggs
1/4 cup butter or margarine, melted
2 cups applesauce, heated

Cheese Filling:
1-1/2 cups uncreamed cottage cheese (12-oz.)
   or 1-1/2 cups Farm-Style Buttermilk
   Cheese, page 18
1 egg

2 tablespoons sugar
1/2 teaspoon vanilla extract
1/8 teaspoon ground cinnamon

Prepare Cheese Filling; set aside. Combine flour and salt in a medium bowl. Beat in milk and eggs until batter is smooth. Preheat a 6-inch skillet or crepe pan over medium heat. Brush lightly with melted butter or margarine. Pour in 2 tablespoons batter. Quickly tilt skillet from side to side to spread batter evenly over bottom. Cook only on 1 side until golden brown on bottom, 2 minutes or less. Loosen with the tip of a knife and slide onto paper towels to drain. Repeat with remaining batter, using additional butter or margarine as needed. Spread crepes out on a flat surface, browned side up. Spoon filling equally onto center of each. Fold 2 sides toward center, not overlapping. Roll up to enclose filling. Add additional butter or margarine to skillet. Lightly brown blintzes on both sides. To serve, spoon hot applesauce over blintzes. Makes 12 blintzes or 6 servings.

Cheese Filling:
In a small bowl, beat cottage cheese or Farm-Style Buttermilk Cheese, egg, sugar, vanilla and cinnamon until combined. Makes about 2 cups.

Shirred Eggs Swiss-Style

Baked or shirred eggs are easy to prepare for a crowd if you have large muffin tins.

6 tablespoons light cream or half-and-half
12 eggs
2 tablespoons butter or margarine,
   room temperature

1-1/2 cups shredded Swiss cheese (6 oz.)
Salt and white pepper to taste
1/4 cup snipped chives

Preheat oven to 325°F (165°C). Butter six 10-ounce ramekins or other individual ovenproof dishes. In each ramekin, layer 1 tablespoon light cream or half-and-half, 2 eggs, 1 teaspoon butter or margarine and 1/4 cup shredded cheese. Sprinkle each with salt and white pepper to taste. Bake about 15 minutes in preheated oven until eggs are set as desired. Sprinkle each dish with 2 teaspoons chives. Serve at once. Makes 6 servings.

Viennese Crepes

Club soda is the special ingredient in these thin, tender pancakes.

3 eggs
1 cup milk
1 teaspoon sugar
1-1/2 cups all-purpose flour
1/4 cup butter or margarine, melted

1 cup club soda
1 (1-lb. 4-oz.) can sliced apples,
    drained, chopped
2 cups dairy sour cream
3 cups shredded Swiss cheese (12 oz.)

Beat eggs, milk, sugar and flour in a medium bowl until blended. Let stand at room temperature 30 minutes. Preheat oven to 300°F (150°C). Place a 7-inch crepe pan or skillet over medium heat. Lightly brush with butter or margarine. Stir club soda into batter. Immediately spoon 2 generous tablespoons crepe batter into pan. Quickly tip pan to swirl batter evenly over bottom. Cook crepe until lightly browned, 2 to 3 minutes. Use a turner to loosen edges and turn crepe. Lightly brown other side. Stack crepes on an oven-proof platter. Cover and keep warm in preheated oven. Cook remaining batter, adding butter or margarine as needed. Remove crepes from oven. Turn oven temperature to 350°F (175°C). Lightly butter a 9" x 9" baking dish; set aside. Place apples in a medium bowl. Stir in sour cream. Spread crepes out on a flat surface. Spoon 2 tablespoons filling across one side of each crepe. Sprinkle each with 2 tablespoons cheese. Roll up crepes around filling and place in prepared baking dish. Spoon remaining filling evenly around crepes. Sprinkle with remaining cheese. Bake until crepes are warm and cheese is very soft, about 10 minutes. Makes 16 crepes.

Variation

Spicy Crepes: Add 1/2 teaspoon ground cinnamon and 1/8 teaspoon ground nutmeg to the filling.

Tuscany-Style Scrambled Eggs

Serve this sausage-rich dish with melon and thick-sliced Italian whole-wheat bread.

1 lb. hot Italian sausages, casings removed
1/4 cup chopped onion
1/4 cup chopped green pepper
1 (16-oz.) can whole tomatoes, undrained
1 (4-oz.) can mushroom stems and pieces,
    drained
2 teaspoons sugar

1/2 teaspoon dried oregano leaves, crumbled
1/2 teaspoon salt
8 eggs, slightly beaten
2-1/4 cups shredded mozzarella cheese (9 oz.)
Salt and black pepper to taste
Parsley sprigs, if desired

Place sausage, onion and green pepper in a medium skillet over medium heat. Cook until sausage is no longer pink. Remove drippings from skillet. Add tomatoes with liquid, mushroom stems and pieces, sugar, oregano and 1/2 teaspoon salt. Simmer until most of the liquid evaporates, about 10 minutes. Add eggs and 1-3/4 cups cheese. Stir over low heat until cheese melts and eggs are set as desired, about 10 minutes. Season with salt and black pepper to taste. Spoon into a warm serving bowl. Sprinkle with remaining cheese. Garnish with parsley sprigs, if desired. Makes 6 servings.

Double-Delight Omelet

Swirl the butter or margarine over the sides and bottom as you tip the pan.

1 cup cream-style cottage cheese (8 oz.)

1 tablespoon snipped fresh or
  freeze-dried chives

2 tablespoons finely diced celery

2 teaspoons snipped fresh parsley or
  dried parsley leaves

1 tablespoon milk

Salt to taste

4 eggs

1/2 teaspoon salt

1/8 teaspoon white pepper

1 tablespoon butter or margarine

1/2 cup shredded Colby or Longhorn cheese
  (2 oz.)

Combine cottage cheese, chives, celery, parsley and milk in a small bowl. Add salt to taste; set aside. In another small bowl, beat eggs slightly with 1/2 teaspoon salt and white pepper. Melt butter or margarine in a 10-inch omelet pan or skillet over medium heat. Add eggs. Stir with the back of a fork held flat on the bottom of pan. While stirring, slide pan briskly back and forth over heat until omelet is set on bottom and slightly soft on top. Remove from heat. Sprinkle omelet with shredded cheese. Spoon cottage cheese mixture down center. Fold 1/3 of omelet over cottage cheese mixture. With a spatula, slide omelet onto a warm platter. Fold remaining 1/3 over. Makes 2 servings.

How to Make
Double-Delight Omelet

1/Stir egg mixture with back of fork held flat on bottom of pan until omelet is slightly set.

2/Use a spatula to fold 1 side of omelet over cheese mixture, then slide omelet onto a warm platter.

Longhorn Baked Eggs

Ramekins are casserole dishes small enough for individual servings.

1 cup dairy sour cream
1/4 cup milk
1/2 teaspoon salt

2 drops hot pepper sauce
6 oz. Longhorn cheese, cut in 6 slices
6 eggs

Preheat oven to 350°F (175°C). Butter six 10-ounce ramekins or other ovenproof dishes; set aside. In a small bowl, combine sour cream, milk, salt and hot pepper sauce. Place 1 slice of cheese in each ramekin. Top each with 1 egg. Spoon sour cream mixture equally around each egg. Bake about 15 minutes in preheated oven until eggs are set as desired. Makes 6 servings.

Variations

Hearty Baked Eggs: Over each cheese slice, place 1 tomato slice sprinkled with salt and pepper. Break eggs onto tomato slices. Proceed as directed above.

Canadian Baked Eggs: Place 1 thin slice of lightly browned Canadian bacon or 2 slices bacon cooked crisp and crumbled in each dish before adding cheese. Proceed as directed above.

Tilsit Potato Pancakes

Rhubarb sauce is supposed to be tart, but if you like yours sweeter, add more sugar.

Fresh Rhubarb Sauce, see below
3 eggs
4 medium potatoes, peeled, shredded
1 cup shredded Tilsit cheese (4 oz.)
1/4 cup minced onion

2 tablespoons all-purpose flour
1 teaspoon salt
1/8 teaspoon pepper
Oil for frying

Fresh Rhubarb Sauce:
2 lb. fresh rhubarb, cut in 1-inch pieces
2/3 cup water

1/2 cup sugar
1/2 teaspoon nutmeg

Prepare Fresh Rhubarb Sauce; set aside. Use a fork to beat eggs in a large bowl. Stir in potatoes, cheese, onion, flour, salt and pepper. Pour enough oil into a large skillet to coat the bottom. Place over medium-high heat. Pour batter into skillet about 1/4 cup at a time, 1 inch apart. Use the back of a spoon to spread batter evenly into 3-inch cakes. Cook until golden brown and crisp on one side, 2 to 3 minutes. Turn and cook other side. Add more oil if needed. Drain on paper towels. Serve immediately with sauce. Makes about 12 pancakes.

Fresh Rhubarb Sauce:
Combine rhubarb and water in a medium saucepan. Boil over medium heat 4 to 5 minutes, stirring occasionally. Stir in sugar and nutmeg. Pour into a medium bowl; chill. Makes 3 cups.

Nachos in the Morning

Change the garnish to mashed avocado, sliced green onions, chopped peanuts or salsa.

1 cup dairy sour cream
1 (2-1/4-oz.) can sliced ripe olives, drained
1/2 lb. bulk pork sausage
1 small onion, chopped

1 (4-oz.) can chopped green chiles, drained
About 4 cups crisp small corn chips
2 cups shredded Monterey Jack cheese (8 oz.)
8 eggs

Stir sour cream until smooth. Spoon into a small serving dish; set aside. Place drained olives in a second small serving dish; set aside. Crumble sausage into a cold medium skillet. Add onion. Stir over medium-high heat until sausage is browned. Stir in green chiles. Remove from heat. Divide corn chips among four 10-ounce ramekins or other small ovenproof dishes. With a slotted spoon, evenly divide sausage mixture among ramekins. Sprinkle 1/4 cup of the cheese over sausage mixture in each ramekin. Set aside. Pour all but 1 tablespoon drippings from skillet. Break eggs into skillet. Stir constantly over low heat until eggs are set. Preheat broiler to 425°F (220°C). Divide scrambled eggs among ramekins. Top with remaining cheese. Broil 3 to 5 inches from heat until cheese melts, 2 to 3 minutes. Serve immediately with sour cream and ripe olives for garnishes. Makes 4 servings.

How to Make Nachos in the Morning

1/Use a slotted spoon to place sausage mixture over corn chips in heat resistant dishes.

2/Top each with 1/4 cup shredded cheese. Spoon scrambled eggs into dishes.

Streusel Coffeecake

Powdered sugar is also called confectioner's sugar.

1/4 cup butter or margarine
2 tablespoons granulated sugar
3/4 teaspoon salt
1/2 cup milk
1 pkg. active dry yeast (1 tablespoon)
1/4 cup warm water (about 110°F, 45°C)

2 eggs
About 3-1/4 cups all-purpose flour
Cheese Filling, see below
Crumb Topping, see below
Powdered sugar

Cheese Filling:
2 (8-oz.) pkgs. cream cheese,
    room temperature
1 cup packed light brown sugar

2 eggs
2 teaspoons vanilla extract
3/4 cup golden raisins

Crumb Topping:
1-1/4 cups all-purpose flour
1/2 cup powdered sugar
1 teaspoon baking powder

1/2 teaspoon ground cinnamon
1/2 cup butter or margarine

Melt butter or margarine in a small saucepan over low heat. Stir in granulated sugar, salt and milk. Heat milk mixture to lukewarm, about 105°F (40°C). In a large bowl, sprinkle yeast over warm water. Let stand until softened. Beat eggs and cooled milk mixture into yeast mixture by hand or with electric mixer on low speed. Add 2 cups of the flour. Beat by hand or with electric mixer on medium speed 3 minutes until batter pulls away from side of bowl. With a spoon, stir in about 1 cup of the flour to make a soft dough. Add more flour if needed. Turn dough out on a lightly floured surface. Let rest 8 to 10 minutes. Clean and butter bowl; set aside. Knead dough until smooth and satiny, about 10 minutes. Place dough in bowl. Turn dough to butter all sides. Cover and let rise in a warm place free from drafts until nearly doubled in bulk, about 45 minutes. Prepare Cheese Filling and Crumb Topping. Butter a 14-inch pizza pan or a 15-1/2" x 10" baking sheet with raised edges. Punch dough down. Turn out onto prepared pan. Cover with bowl and let stand 10 minutes. Gently pat out dough to edge of pan. Cover evenly with Cheese Filling. Sprinkle evenly with Crumb Topping. Let rise until puffed, about 20 minutes. Preheat oven to 375°F (190°C). Bake 25 minutes in preheated oven until crust and topping are golden brown. Let cool 20 minutes before serving. Dust with powdered sugar. To freeze, cool completely and wrap in heavy foil. To reheat, thaw at room temperature, loosely cover with foil and warm in preheated 350°F (175°C) oven 15 minutes. Makes 14 to 16 servings.

Cheese Filling:
Beat cream cheese with electric mixer on medium-high speed or by hand until fluffy. Beat in brown sugar, eggs and vanilla. Stir in raisins.

Crumb Topping:
Combine flour, powdered sugar, baking powder and cinnamon in a medium bowl. Cut in butter or margarine with a pastry blender or 2 knives until coarse, crumbs form.

Snacks & Starters

Snacks are appropriate for all occasions—early morning, between meals, after meals, with guests, at bedtime and in the middle of the night. Snacks are intended to keep away hunger pangs or to stir up interest when conversation lags.

Brie is an excellent cheese to use in snacks and starters and is used in Brie in a Braid. It is soft, creamy and tantalizingly pungent. Brie, a surface-ripened cheese, should be eaten at the just-ripe-enough but not-too-ripe moment. The edible crust should bulge slightly at the sides and feel soft when you press with your fingers. The aroma should be pungent, but never strong with ammonia, which indicates over-ripe cheese.

John Bull's Potted Cheshire is a make-ahead spread that will keep two weeks in your refrigerator. Spreads or dips should be stored in airtight containers with very little air-space to prevent drying and mold growth. In this spread, British *Cheshire* cheese is spiced, peppered and sherried for glorious flavor.

Hors d'oeuvres, canapés and appetizers are lumped under the general heading *starters*. Their purpose is to get a party or meal or any get-together started.

In Mauna Loa Cheese Bites, chutney is combined with *cream* cheese, *blue* cheese and *Cheddar* cheese. Chutney was originally an Indian condiment made with spices and local fruit, such as mangoes and raisins. Today chutney is used world wide and is found in the specialty section of your supermarket. Or you can make your own using the recipe with Port Salut Roll, page 35.

Caviar is an exotic and rather expensive ingredient sometimes used in snacks and starters. Black Pearl Treasure makes caviar go a long way. Fresh caviar is expensive because it can't be frozen for transporting. It must be iced when left at room temperature for even an hour. Because it's so perishable, methods of pasteurizing and canning caviar were developed. This brought down the price so more people could enjoy this delicious snack. Glass jars of caviar need not be refrigerated until they are opened. Black caviar is suggested for this recipe, although you may use another kind.

Teenagers' Snack Party
Mugs of Hot Black Bean Soup
John Bull's Potted Cheshire, page 36
Festive Pretzels, page 42
Homemade Liptauer, page 44
Party Pumpernickel
Raw Vegetable Relish Tray
Merlin's Magic Cupcakes, page 116

Port Salut Roll

Use the chutney lavishly if you like, but go easy with the mustard dip—it is very hot.

2 eggs
1/2 teaspoon salt
1/4 cup all-purpose flour
1/2 cup milk
2 tablespoons butter or margarine
Chutney, see below, or
   2 (10-1/2-oz.) jars chutney

Port Salut Filling, see below
1/2 cup dry mustard
Hot water
1/2 cup snipped fresh parsley
1/2 cup freshly grated Romano cheese
   (1-1/2-oz.)

Chutney:

1 (12-oz.) jar peach preserves
2 tablspoons lemon juice
2 tablespoons white vinegar
2 tablespoons hot water
1/4 cup chopped candied ginger
2-inch piece cinnamon stick

6 whole cloves
1/2 cup dried currants
1/2 teaspoon celery seeds
1/2 teaspoon mustard seeds
3 drops hot pepper sauce

Port Salut Filling:

6 thinly sliced green onions
1/4 lb. frozen tiny shrimp, thawed
1 cup slivered prosciutto ham
1/4 cup slivered water chestnuts

6 oz. Port Salut cheese, finely chopped
Salt and pepper to taste
2 tablespoons olive oil
2-1/2 teaspoons lemon juice

Preheat oven to 350°F (175°C). In a small bowl, beat eggs slightly. Add salt, flour and milk. Beat until smooth. In a heavy 10- or 12-inch skillet with an ovenproof handle, heat butter or margarine until bubbling. Pour in egg mixture. Bake in preheated oven about 25 minutes until browned and set; keep warm. While egg mixture bakes, prepare Chutney and Port Salut Filling. To make mustard dip, mix mustard with just enough hot water to make a smooth, thin paste; set aside. Loosen egg wrapper from skillet with a spatula and place on a platter. Spread with Port Salut Filling; roll up jelly-roll fashion. Turn seam-side down. Brush top with oil-lemon juice mixture reserved from Port Salut Filling. Combine snipped parsley and Romano cheese in a small bowl; sprinkle over roll. Slice and serve immediately with Chutney and mustard dip. Makes 10 to 12 appetizer servings.

Chutney:
Combine all ingredients in a medium saucepan. Cover and simmer 10 minutes. Uncover and simmer 5 minutes longer, stirring often to prevent scorching. Keep warm. Spoon into a warm serving dish.

Port Salut Filling:
Place green onions, shrimp, prosciutto ham, water chestnuts and Port Salut cheese in a large bowl. Toss to combine; add salt and pepper to taste. Combine olive oil and lemon juice in a small bowl. Spoon 5 teaspoons of juice mixture over filling; toss to coat.

John Bull's Potted Cheshire

For the best flavor, refrigerate at least 24 hours before serving.

4 cups shredded Cheshire cheese (1 lb.)
3 drops hot pepper sauce
6 tablespoons butter or margarine,
   room temperature

1/2 teaspoon ground mace
1/8 teaspoon dry mustard
1/2 cup cream sherry

In a medium bowl, combine ingredients in order given. With a slotted spoon, beat until smooth. Pack into a 2-cup crock or jar with an airtight lid. Press waxed paper down onto cheese mixture; cover with lid. Will keep 2 weeks in refrigerator. Makes 2 cups.

Variation

John Bull's Herbed Potted Cheshire: Substitute 1/4 cup fresh sage or parsley leaves for mace. Bruise herb in a mortar and pestle or in a cup with the back of a spoon; add to cheese mixture.

Black Pearl Treasure

Salted, pasteurized or pressed caviar keeps longer than fresh caviar and is less expensive.

6 hard-cooked eggs, peeled
3 tablespoons mayonnaise
1-1/2 cups minced onions
1 (8-oz.) pkg. cream cheese,
   room temperature

2/3 cup dairy sour cream
1 (3-1/2-oz.) jar caviar
12 lemon wedges
12 small parsley sprigs

Generously butter an 8-inch springform pan; set aside. Chop eggs; combine with mayonnaise in a medium bowl. Spread egg mixture over bottom of prepared pan. Evenly distribute onions over egg mixture. Blend cream cheese and sour cream in a small bowl until smooth. Dip a spatula in water and use to spread cream cheese mixture over onions. Cover pan and refrigerate at least 3 hours or overnight. Just before serving, spread caviar evenly over cream cheese mixture. Run the blade of a knife around inside of pan. Remove side of pan. Arrange lemon wedges and parsley sprigs in center like wheel spokes. Cut in wedges to serve. Makes 12 appetizer servings.

Before you buy rye flour, check the label. Some rye flours contain crushed caraway seeds. If the recipe also calls for caraway seeds, as in Brie in a Braid, page 37, the caraway flavor may be too strong.

Easy Breadsticks

With French bread in the freezer, you can make these in no time at all.

1/2 cup butter or margarine
1/4 cup finely snipped fresh parsley
1 teaspoon paprika

3/4 cup freshly grated Parmesan cheese
  (2-1/4-oz.)
1 long thin loaf French bread

Preheat oven to 400°F (205°C). In a small bowl, stir butter or margarine until smooth. Stir in parsley; set aside. Combine paprika and Parmesan cheese in a small bowl; set aside. Cut bread crosswise in thirds. Split each third in half to make 6 pieces. Cut each piece lengthwise into thirds to make 18 pieces. Spread butter or margarine mixture lightly on cut sides of bread. Place on a large ungreased baking sheet. Sprinkle with cheese mixture. Bake about 5 minutes in preheated oven until crisp and golden. Serve immediately. Makes 18 appetizer servings.

Variation

Easy Herb Sticks: Substitute 1/4 cup finely snipped fresh dillweed or basil or 1 tablespoon crumbled dried dillweed or basil for parsley. Substitute Romano cheese for Parmesan cheese.

Brie in a Braid

Brie cheese comes in three strengths, young *or* mild, mature *and* ripe.

2-1/2 cups warm water (110°F, 45°C)
2 pkgs. active dry yeast (2 tablespoons)
1 tablespoon sugar
1 tablespoon salt
2 tablespoons butter or margarine,
  room temperature
3 cups rye flour

4 to 5 cups all-purpose flour
1 tablespoon caraway seeds, if desired
1 egg, beaten
1 tablespoon milk
1 wheel Brie cheese,
  about 8 inches in diameter (about 2 lbs.)

Warm a large bowl by rinsing with hot water; dry. Pour warm water into bowl. Sprinkle in yeast; stir until dissolved. Add sugar, salt, butter or margarine, rye flour, 1 cup all-purpose flour and caraway seeds, if desired. Beat until smooth. Add about 3 cups of the remaining all-purpose flour to make a stiff dough. Turn out on a lightly floured surface; let rest 5 minutes. While dough rests, clean and grease bowl; set aside. Knead dough until smooth and elastic, 8 to 10 minutes. Place dough in prepared bowl. Turn to grease all sides. Cover and let rise in a warm place free from drafts until doubled in bulk, about 1 hour. Punch down dough and divide into 3 equal parts. Roll each part between your hands to make a rope about 30 inches long. Braid ropes. Butter a large baking sheet and the outside of an 8-inch round baking pan. Invert baking pan on center of baking sheet. Arrange braided dough around pan. Pinch ends of braid together. Cover and let rise 35 minutes. Preheat oven to 375°F (190°C). Combine egg and milk in a small bowl; gently brush over top of braid. Bake 40 minutes in preheated oven until brown and crusty. Remove from baking sheet; gently remove center pan. Cool on rack. To serve, place cheese in center of a large round platter or tray. Place braid around cheese. Makes about 20 appetizer servings.

Stuffed Edam

Pile the satiny-smooth filling into the bright red wax cheese shell.

1 (about 30-oz.) whole Edam cheese,
   room temperature
1/4 cup butter or margarine,
   room temperature
1/2 teaspoon dry mustard
1/4 cup chopped pimiento-stuffed olives

1/8 teaspoon hot pepper sauce
2 teaspoons instant minced onion
2-1/2 teaspoons dry white wine
1 teaspoon caraway seeds or
   1/2 teaspoon dillweed or celery seeds
Assorted crackers

Cut off top of cheese. Scoop out inside, leaving a 1/4-inch wall of cheese inside wax shell. Shred scooped out cheese onto waxed paper. In a blender or food processor, combine shredded cheese, butter or margarine, mustard, olives, hot pepper sauce, onion, wine and caraway, dillweed or celery seeds. Process until smooth. Pack cheese mixture lightly into shell. Serve immediately or refrigerate until 30 minutes before serving. To serve, place filled shell on a large platter or tray; surround with crackers. Makes about 1-1/2 cups.

How to Make Stuffed Edam

1/Scoop cheese from center of cheese ball, leaving a 1/4-inch shell.

2/Process cheese mixture until smooth, then pack lightly into shell.

Mauna Loa Cheese Bites

If the fruit pieces in your chutney are large, chop them before measuring.

1 (8-oz.) pkg. cream cheese,
   room temperature
1 cup crumbled blue cheese (4 oz.)

2 cups shredded sharp Cheddar cheese (8 oz.)
1/4 cup chopped chutney
1 cup finely chopped macadamia nuts

In a large bowl, beat cream cheese until smooth and fluffy. Beat in blue and Cheddar cheeses. Gently blend in chutney by hand. Refrigerate until mixture can be easily handled, at least 1 hour. Shape by teaspoonfuls into small balls. Roll cheese balls in nuts. Serve immediately or refrigerate until serving time. Makes about 72 cheese balls.

Turkish Turnarounds

Serve these feather-light little pastries with One-Pot Wonder, page 72.

2 (3-oz.) pkgs. cream cheese with chives,
   room temperature
2 tablespoons grated Parmesan cheese
1 teaspoon Worcestershire sauce

2 drops hot pepper sauce
2 (8-oz.) pkgs. refrigerated crescent dinner
   rolls

Preheat oven to 375°F (190°C). In a small bowl, combine cream cheese, Parmesan cheese, Worcestershire sauce and hot pepper sauce. Set aside. Unroll dinner rolls. Do not separate at perforations. On a lightly floured surface, pat out each of the 8 pieces to make eight 6" x 4" rectangles. Cut each rectangle in half crosswise to make sixteen 4" x 3" rectangles. Spread 2 teaspoons of the cheese mixture evenly over each rectangle. Roll up jelly-roll fashion. Place seam-side down on a large ungreased baking sheet. With tines of a fork, press ends of each roll firmly to seal. Bake 15 minutes in preheated oven until lightly browned. Serve immediately. Makes 16 pastries.

Addie's Popcorn

Grandmother Addie keeps her cookie jar filled with this delicious sugarfree snack.

3 qts. freshly popped corn
3/4 cup shredded Cheddar cheese (3 oz.)
1/3 cup butter or margarine

1/2 teaspoon salt
1/4 teaspoon hot pepper sauce

Preheat oven to 300°F (150°C). Place popped corn in a large, shallow 4-quart baking pan. Add cheese; toss to combine. Melt butter or margarine in a small saucepan. Stir in salt and hot pepper sauce; heat 1 minute. Slowly pour over popcorn mixture, tossing lightly to mix well. Bake 15 minutes in preheated oven until hot and crisp. Serve immediately or store in an airtight container up to 2 weeks. Makes about 3 quarts.

Camembert Kisses

These kisses are best when hot, but delicious when cold.

3/4 lb. Camembert cheese,
   cut into 24 wedge-shaped pieces
4 eggs

1-1/2 cups fine dry breadcrumbs, page 108
Vegetable oil for deep-frying

Keep cheese refrigerated until needed. Lightly beat eggs in a small bowl. Spread breadcrumbs on waxed paper. Quickly coat cheese wedges with eggs, then with breadcrumbs. Repeat coatings. Place kisses 1/2 inch apart on a large baking sheet or platter. Refrigerate at least 2 hours. In a deep-fryer or large saucepan, pour oil at least 2 inches deep. Heat to 375°F (190°C). At this temperature a 1-inch cube of bread will turn golden brown in 40 seconds. With a slotted spoon, lower a few kisses at a time into hot oil. Cook until golden brown; drain on paper towels. Serve immediately. Makes 24 appetizer servings.

Roquefort Puffs

Serve these little puffs soon after you fill them so they will remain crisp.

24 Gruyère Puffs from Gougère, page 41
1/2 cup butter or margarine,
   room temperature
1 cup crumbled Roquefort cheese (4 oz.)

2 tablespoons port wine
3 tablespoons chopped toasted almonds
48 watercress leaves
Watercress sprigs

Slice tops from puffs, keeping each puff with its own top. Combine butter, cheese and port wine in a medium bowl. Beat until smooth and fluffy. Stir in almonds. Put 1 generous teaspoonful of filling into each puff. Place tops slightly to one side over filling. Tuck 2 watercress leaves into filling on open side of each puff. Arrange puffs on a platter. Garnish with watercress sprigs. Makes 24 appetizer servings.

Serbian Snack Cheese

Black peppercorns can be cracked in a pepper mill at the table, or purchased coarse or fine ground.

2 cups unsalted butter
2 cups crumbled feta cheese (8 oz.)
1 cup Rich Cream-Style Cheese, page 16, or
   1 (8-oz.) pkg. cream cheese

1/4 cup cracked black peppercorns
Thinly sliced party-style dark
   pumpernickel bread

Place butter and cheeses in blender or food processor. Process until smooth. Shape into a mound on a small platter. Sprinkle with peppercorns and surround with bread slices. Makes about 5 cups.

Hot Cheddar Puffs

Bring in your electric fryer and cook these delectable hors d'oeuvres to order.

3 eggs, separated
1-1/2 cups shredded sharp Cheddar cheese
  (6 oz.)
1 tablespoon all-purpose flour
1/4 teaspoon salt

3 drops hot pepper sauce
1 tablespoon water
3/4 cup fine cracker crumbs
Oil for deep-frying

In a small bowl, beat egg whites until stiff. In a medium bowl, combine cheese, flour, salt and hot pepper sauce. Beat in stiff egg whites by hand or with electric mixer at low speed. In a small bowl, beat egg yolks and water until just blended. Spread out creacker crumbs on waxed paper. Drop cheese mixture by tablespoonfuls into crumbs; roll in crumbs to form balls. Roll in egg-yolk mixture to cover completely; return to crumbs and coat completely. Place 1/2 inch apart on a baking sheet or large platter. Refrigerate at least 2 hours. In deep-fryer or large saucepan, pour oil at least 2 inches deep. Heat to 375°F (190°C). At this temperature a 1-inch cube of bread will turn golden brown in 40 seconds. With a slotted spoon, lower a few balls at a time into hot oil. Cook until golden brown; drain on paper towels. Serve immediately. Makes 24 appetizer servings.

Gougère

Split and fill with a creamed chicken or creamed ham mixture, to make a delicious main dish.

1 cup boiling water
1/2 cup butter or margarine
1 cup all-purpose flour
1/2 teaspoon salt
4 eggs

1 cup shredded Gruyère cheese (4 oz.)
2 tablespoons mayonnaise
2 tablespoons grated Parmesan cheese
1 teaspoon paprika

Preheat oven to 400°F (205°C). Heat water and butter or margarine in a medium saucepan until water boils and butter or margarine melts. Add flour and salt all at once; reduce heat. Stir vigorously until mixture leaves side of pan and begins to form a ball. Remove from heat. Add eggs one at a time, beating well after each addition. Continue to beat until mixture has a satiny sheen. Stir in Gruyère cheese. On a large ungreased baking sheet, spoon dough into two 1-1/2-inch-wide strips, 4 inches apart. Bake 45 to 50 minutes in preheated oven until golden brown and firm to the touch. Remove from oven. Prick both sides of strips in several places with a sharp fork. Brush tops of strips lightly with mayonnaise. In a small bowl, combine Parmesan cheese and paprika. Sprinkle over mayonnaise. Turn off oven and return strips to oven 5 minutes longer. To serve, cut in 1-inch slices. Makes about 24 servings.

Variation

Gruyère Puffs: With 2 spoons or a pastry bag with a plain tube, drop Gougère mixture into small puffs on an ungreased baking sheet. Bake about 25 minutes in a preheated 425°F (220°C) oven. Serve plain or cool slightly and split. Fill with ham or chicken salad or a cheese mixture; see Roquefort Puffs, page 40. Makes about 16 puffs.

Festive Pretzels

Crumbling dried leaf herbs brings out more flavor.

1/2 cup butter or margarine	1/2 teaspoon dried basil leaves, crumbled
1 cup all-purpose flour	1/4 teaspoon dried oregano leaves, crumbled
2 tablespoons grated Parmesan cheese	1/4 teaspoon dried rosemary leaves, crumbled
1 cup shredded sharp Cheddar cheese (4 oz.)	About 3 tablespoons cold water
1/2 teaspoon garlic powder	Paprika, if desired
1/2 teaspoon onion powder	

In a medium bowl, cut butter or margarine into flour with a pastry blender or 2 knives until mixture looks like fine breadcrumbs. Stir in Parmesan cheese, Cheddar cheese, garlic powder, onion powder, basil, oregano and rosemary. Sprinkle cold water over mixture 1 tablespoon at a time. Toss with a fork until dough gathers into a ball. Divide dough into 24 equal balls. Cover and refrigerate 20 to 30 minutes until firm. Preheat oven to 425°F (220°C). On a lightly floured surface, roll each ball into a thin rope about 11 inches long. Lay on an ungreased baking sheet. Twist into pretzel shapes and arrange about 3/4 inch apart. Sprinkle lightly with paprika, if desired. Bake 12 to 15 minutes in preheated oven until golden. Cool on racks. Serve the same day or wrap airtight and freeze. Recrisp by baking frozen pretzels in a preheated 350°F (175°C) oven about 6 minutes. Serve immediately. Makes 2 dozen.

How to Shape Festive Pretzels

1/Roll balls of dough into thin 11-inch ropes.

2/Lay ropes on baking sheet; twist into pretzels.

Quick Swiss Stack-Ups

Serve these crisp, flavorful stacks with Dutch Apple Soup, page 49.

1 (11-oz.) pkg. pie crust mix
Water
1/4 cup butter or margarine,
   room temperature

2 cups shredded Swiss cheese (8 oz.)
Paprika

Preheat oven to 400°F (205°C). Grease a large baking sheet; set aside. Prepare pie crust mix with water according to package directions. On a lightly floured surface, roll out to a 20" x 12" rectangle. Cut crosswise into five 12" x 4" strips. Spread strips evenly with butter or margarine. Sprinkle 4 strips evenly with cheese and paprika. Stack strips alternately beginning with a cheese topped strip. Place final strip buttered-side down. Press firmly together. Cut in half lengthwise making two 12" x 2" layered strips. Cut into 1/2-inch wide slices. Place 2 inches apart on prepared baking sheet. Bake 12 to 15 minutes in preheated oven until golden. Makes 48 stacks.

Variations

Add poppy seeds, celery seeds or toasted sesame seeds to the shredded Swiss cheese.

Substitute onion powder or garlic powder to taste for the paprika.

Quick & Easy Snacks

• Soften cream cheese with a little milk or cream. Season with garlic juice or powder. Spread on slices of dried beef; roll up.
• Make a half-and-half mixture of Neufchâtel and blue cheese. Moisten with a little sour cream. Use to stuff 2-inch pieces of celery.
• On a wooden pick or skewer, spear 1 sharp Cheddar cheese cube, 1 pickled cocktail onion, 1 small stuffed olive, another onion and another cheese cube.
• Soften cream cheese with a little milk or cream. Season with onion powder and curry powder to taste. Use as a dip for unpeeled apple wedges.
• Mix crumbled blue cheese with milk or cream to make a thick spread. Pit and halve fresh sweet cherries. Fill cherry halves with spread. Press the halves back together.
• Add sour cream to shredded Monterey Jack cheese to make a thick spread. Remove casings from thin slices of salami or another highly flavored sausage. Stack sausage 6 slices high with filling between slices. Cut sausage stacks in wedges to serve.
• Season softened cream cheese liberally with snipped chives. Use to stuff individual blades of Belgian endive.
• Combine shredded brick cheese with minced onion, green pepper and pimiento. Bind with a little mayonnaise if necessary. Use to stuff hollowed-out cherry tomatoes.
• Season shredded Muenster cheese with hot pepper sauce, Worcestershire sauce and garlic juice. Moisten with enough soft butter to hold mixture together. Roll into balls; roll the balls in finely chopped walnuts.
• Process 2 cups cottage cheese in blender until smooth. Spread on toast. Top with one or more of the following: cinnamon sugar, strawberry or raspberry jam, thinly sliced green onions, chopped radishes, poppy seeds or toasted sesame seeds, snipped chives or parsley, alfalfa or bean sprouts, crumbled crisp bacon or chopped seeded cucumbers.

Homemade Liptauer

Beautiful rose-gold Hungarian paprika is sold as sweet, half-sweet *and* hot—*all great flavors.*

1 cup Rich Cream-Style Cheese, page 16, or
   1 (8-oz.) pkg. cream cheese
1/4 cup unsalted butter
3 tablespoons dairy sour cream
1 tablespoon minced onion
4 anchovy fillets, drained, minced

1 teaspoon dry mustard
1 teaspoon caraway seeds
1 teaspoon Hungarian hot paprika
Salt and white pepper to taste
Poppy seed crackers or sesame seed crackers

Place cheese, butter, sour cream, onion, anchovies, mustard, caraway seeds and paprika in blender or food processor. Process until mixture is smooth. Season with salt and white pepper to taste. Spoon lightly into a small bowl. Place on a tray or platter and surround with crackers. Makes about 1-1/2 cups dip.

Liptauer in Pumpernickel

Make the cheese mixture two days in advance so the exquisite flavors will have time to mellow.

2 (8-oz.) pkgs. cream cheese,
   room temperature
1 (3-oz.) pkg. cream cheese,
   room temperature
1-1/2 cups shredded sharp Cheddar cheese
   (6 oz.)
2 teaspoons Dijon-style mustard

2 tablespoons chopped onion
5 tablespoons butter or margarine,
   room temperature
Paprika
1 (14-inch) round loaf pumpernickel bread
Garnishes, see below

Garnishes:
2 (2-oz.) cans fillets of anchovies, drained,
   coarsely chopped
2/3 cup thinly sliced green onions
2/3 cup coarsely chopped seeded cucumber

2/3 cup thinly sliced radishes
1/2 cup drained capers
Thinly sliced pumpernickel bread

Place cream cheese, Cheddar cheese, mustard, onion and butter or margarine in blender or food processor. Process until smooth. Stir in paprika to give a rosy glow. Cover and refrigerate 2 days. On serving day, cut 1 round slice about 9 inches in diameter from top of pumpernickel loaf. Cut slice into 1-1/2-inch squares; set aside. Pull out center of loaf in small chunks, leaving a sturdy shell. Lightly toast bread squares and chunks in broiler. Cover lightly; set aside. Prepare garnishes. Place all but sliced pumpernickel in separate small bowls. Cover and refrigerate. Lightly spoon cheese mixture into pumpernickel shell. Cover completely with plastic wrap. Refrigerate 2 hours. Half an hour before serving, unwrap filled shell. Place on a platter and surround with toasted pumpernickel. Place bowls of garnishes and sliced pumpernickel bread nearby. To serve, spread pieces of bread with cheese mixture. Top with desired garnish. Makes 12 to 14 appetizer servings.

Soups, Salads & Sandwiches

Make soups during quiet times such as early mornings or during a Sunday cook-for-the-week binge, and refrigerate or freeze them for later. Be sure to cool soups completely, then cover tightly, label and freeze them. Hot foods cause home freezers to work overtime and encourage the formation of large ice crystals which destroy cell walls in food.

Almost any soup can be stored up to 4 or 5 months in the freezer. Thaw frozen soups in your refrigerator for about 24 hours, then heat them slowly. Never boil cheese soups. Too high a temperature causes fat or oil to separate from the rest of the curd, leaving the cheese tough and stringy.

All cheeses used in soups, sauces or casseroles should be shredded or finely chopped before being stirred into the hot mixture. If the cheese is left in large pieces, it will not melt into a smooth sauce. Of course, if you want unmelted pieces of cheese in your soup, then leave it in one-inch cubes or larger.

Cream soups can be served hot or cold. When heated they tend to curdle. If a cream soup curdles, process it in your blender to make it smooth.

Bottled salad dressings are improved by adding 1/4 to 1/2 cup freshly shredded or grated cheese to one cup of dressing just before serving. Try *Romano* in Italian dressing, *Cheddar* or *Colby* in French, *Monterey Jack* in green goddess, *sapsago* in Russian, *Gruyère* in Thousand Island and *Tilsit* in coleslaw dressing.

Easy Cheese Salad Dressings

Most homemade salad dressings keep well for two weeks refrigerated in jars with tight-fitting lids. Here are some of my favorites.

- **Blue Cheese Vinaigrette:** Combine 2/3 cup vegetable or olive oil, 1/2 cup wine vinegar, 1 teaspoon salt, 1/2 teaspoon sugar, 1/4 teaspoon pepper, 1/3 cup crumbled blue cheese and 1 minced garlic clove. Blend well.
- **Blue Cheese Cream Dressing:** Combine 1/2 cup mayonnaise, 1/2 cup dairy sour cream, 1 tablespoon lemon juice, 1/4 teaspoon salt and 3 drops hot pepper sauce. Blend with a whisk or fork. Stir in 1/2 cup crumbled blue cheese.
- **Parmesan Dressing:** Combine 2/3 cup olive oil, 1/2 cup wine vinegar, 1/2 teaspoon sugar, 1 teaspoon salt, 1/4 teaspoon pepper, 1/2 teaspoon crushed dried basil leaves, 1/2 teaspoon crushed dried tarragon leaves and 2 tablespoons grated Parmesan cheese. Shake well.
- **Rosy Glow Dressing:** In your blender, combine 1 cup whole fresh strawberries, 3/4 cup cream-style cottage cheese, 3 tablespoons lemon juice and 2 tablespoons sugar. Process until smooth. Use on any fruit salad.

Tailgate Picnic
Thermos of Norwegian Onion Soup, page 50
Corn Chips
Mac & Mo to Go, page 51
Italian Sausages & French Rolls
Relish Tray
Fresh Pears

Pictured on the following pages. Clockwise from top left: Corsican Supper Loaf, page 61; Dutch Apple Soup, page 49; Fresh Green Salad with Blue Cheese Cream Dressing, page 45.

Soups

Cheddar Chowder

If the soup is too thick for your taste, thin it with a little extra milk.

6 thick-sliced bacon strips
1/4 cup chopped onion
1/3 cup all-purpose flour
1 qt. milk
2 cups half-and-half or light cream
4 cups shredded sharp Cheddar cheese (1 lb.)

1/2 teaspoon garlic juice
1/2 teaspoon dry mustard
1 teaspoon salt
1/4 teaspoon white pepper
2 tablespoons dried parsley leaves
3/4 cup plain croutons

In a 4-quart pot, cook bacon until crisp. Drain on paper towels; set aside. Reserve about 3 table-spoons bacon drippings in pot. Add onion. Sauté over low heat until tender but not browned. Gradually stir in flour until mixture bubbles and thickens. Stir in milk and cream a little at a time until mixture is smooth. Stir in cheese 1 cup at a time until cheese melts and mixture is smooth. Ladle 1 cup of the soup into a small bowl. Stir in garlic juice, dry mustard, salt, white pepper and parsley leaves. Return to soup in pot, stirring to combine. Simmer 5 minutes. Do not boil. Crumble cooked bacon. Combine with croutons in a small bowl. Ladle soup into soup bowls. Top each serving with about 1 tablespoon bacon-crouton mixture. Serve immediately. Makes 6 to 8 servings.

Cream of Roquefort Milwaukee-Style

This nippy cheese flavor complements the natural sweetness of the vegetables.

1/2 cup butter or margarine
1 large green cabbage, cored, chopped
1 medium cauliflower, separated into cauliflowerets

7 cups chicken broth or stock
1 cup heavy cream or whipping cream
1/2 cup crumbled Roquefort cheese, (2 oz.)
Salt and pepper to taste

Melt butter or margarine in a large saucepan over medium heat. Add cabbage. Stir to coat well. Cook over low heat until tender, about 10 minutes, stirring occasionally. Add cauliflowerets and broth or stock. Bring to a boil; reduce heat. Cover and simmer about 40 minutes until vegetables are very tender. Pour cream into blender or food processor. Add Roquefort cheese. Process at medium speed until smooth. Gradually stir cream mixture into soup. Stir in salt and pepper to taste. Cook until soup is heated through. Do not boil. Serve immediately or refrigerate and serve cold. Makes 8 to 10 servings.

Variations

Cool soup slightly. Process a little at a time in blender or food processor. Reheat puréed soup before serving or refrigerate and serve chilled.

Crumble blue-veined cheeses by pulling them apart with 2 forks. Your fingers are too warm and will make the cheese sticky.

48

Frosty Florentine Cream

In this superior cream of spinach soup, cheese is a delicious substitute for cream.

20 oz. fresh spinach
1/2 cup thinly sliced green onions
3 tablespoons butter or margarine
1/8 teaspoon garlic powder
3 (13-3/4-oz.) cans chicken broth

1/8 teaspoon ground nutmeg
Salt and white pepper to taste
1 (8-oz.) pkg. cream cheese, diced
2 hard-cooked eggs, sieved
2 tablespoons grated Parmesan cheese

Remove tough stems and wilted leaves from spinach. Wash under lukewarm running water. Shake off excess water; set aside. In a large shallow saucepan over medium heat, sauté green onions in butter or margarine until tender but not browned. Stir in garlic powder and rinsed spinach. Cover and cook until spinach wilts, about 10 minutes, stirring occasionally. Add broth. Simmer 5 minutes. Stir in nutmeg and salt and white pepper to taste. Remove from heat. Cool 10 minutes. Purée spinach mixture 1/4 at a time in blender or force through a food mill. Return to saucepan. Add cream cheese. Stir over low heat until cheese melts. Do not boil. Combine sieved eggs and Parmesan cheese in a small bowl. Serve immediately or refrigerate and serve cold. To serve, ladle soup into individual soup bowls. Garnish with sieved egg mixture. Makes 8 servings.

Dutch Apple Soup *Photo on page 47.*

To scald milk, heat without stirring until it steams and the surface begins to quiver.

1/4 cup butter or margarine
1 cup all-purpose flour
2-1/2 cups milk, scalded
3 cups apple cider
3 cups shredded Gouda cheese (12 oz.)
3 egg yolks

1/2 cup heavy cream or whipping cream
1/2 teaspoon salt
1/4 teaspoon ground mace
1/4 cup plain croutons
1 red apple, cored, thinly sliced

Melt butter or margarine in a large saucepan over medium heat. Add 1/2 cup flour. Blend into a smooth paste. Gradually stir in milk until mixture bubbles and thickens. Add apple cider, stirring until blended. Turn heat to lowest setting. Toss Gouda cheese with remaining 1/2 cup flour until coated. Stir into soup a little at a time until cheese melts. In a small bowl, beat egg yolks with a fork until blended. Stir in cream, salt and mace. Stir egg yolk mixture into soup. Heat 5 minutes, stirring constantly. Do not boil. Pour into a soup tureen. Garnish with croutons. Garnish individual servings with apple slices. Serve immediately Makes 6 to 8 servings.

If you substitute dried herb leaves for ground dried herbs, double the amount called for.

Norwegian Onion Soup

Jarlsberg, pronounced YARLS-berg, is similar to Swiss, but milder.

3 tablespoons butter or margarine
3/4 cup thinly sliced green onions with tops
3 tablespoons all-purpose flour

6 cups chicken broth or bouillon
1-1/2 cups shredded Jarlsberg cheese (6 oz.)
Salt and pepper to taste

Melt butter or margarine in a large saucepan over medium heat. Add green onions. Sauté until tender but not browned. Gradually blend in flour. Slowly add broth or bouillon, stirring constantly until mixture thickens and bubbles. Lower heat. Gradually stir in cheese until partially melted. Some shreds of cheese should remain unmelted. Stir in salt and pepper to taste. Serve immediately or refrigerate. Reheat before serving. Makes 4 to 6 servings.

Red & Gold Bisque

When boiled, sour cream curdles and cheese separates.

1/4 cup butter or margarine
1/2 cup finely chopped onion
1 (29-oz.) can tomato purée
2-1/2 cups water

2-1/4 cups shredded extra-sharp or sharp
   Cheddar cheese (9 oz.)
1/2 teaspoon salt
1 cup dairy sour cream

Melt butter or margarine in a large saucepan over medium heat. Add onion. Sauté until tender but not browned. Lower heat. Stir in tomato purée, water, cheese and salt until cheese melts, 10 to 15 minutes. Do not boil. Remove from heat. Let stand 10 minutes. Pour sour cream into a small bowl. Stir in 1 cup of the slightly cooled soup. Gradually stir sour cream mixture into soup until heated through. Do not boil. Makes 6 servings.

Roman Oyster Stew

Freshly grated Romano has a richer flavor and a better texture than the packaged grated cheese.

1/2 cup butter or margarine
2 cups milk
2 cups half-and-half or light cream
3/4 cup freshly grated Romano cheese
   (2-1/4 oz.)

2 tablespoons all-purpose flour
4 slices white bread, toasted
2 tablespoons mayonnaise
2 (8-oz.) cans whole oysters, with liquor

Melt butter or margarine in a large saucepan over medium heat. Stir in milk and cream. Reduce heat to lowest setting. Preheat oven to 350°F (175°C). In a small bowl, toss 1/2 cup of the cheese with flour. Stir cheese mixture into milk mixture until soup begins to bubble. Simmer 5 minutes. Spread toast evenly with mayonnaise. Sprinkle evenly with remaining 1/4 cup cheese. Cut diagonally. Place on an ungreased baking sheet. Bake about 5 minutes in preheated oven until cheese bubbles; set aside. Add oysters with liquor to soup. Continue to cook 2 minutes over low heat. Ladle soup into individual bowls. Float 2 triangles of toast on each serving. Serve immediately. Makes 4 servings.

Alpine Potato-Cheese Soup

A ricer *is a perforated cup with a plunger that forces food through the holes.*

3 tablespoons butter or margarine
1 cup chopped onions
3 large potatoes, peeled, diced
1 teaspoon salt
1/4 teaspoon dry mustard

1/8 teaspoon white pepper
3 cups water
2 cups milk
2 cups shredded Swiss cheese (8 oz.)
2 tablespoons snipped fresh parsley

Melt butter or margarine in a 4-quart saucepan over medium-low heat. Add onion. Sauté until tender but not browned. Stir in potatoes, salt, dry mustard, white pepper and water. Bring to a boil. Cover and reduce heat. Simmer 30 minutes until potatoes are very soft. Press potato mixture through a ricer or a fine sieve into a large bowl. Return to saucepan. Stir in milk. Heat slowly to just boiling. Lower heat slightly. Stir in cheese until melted. Sprinkle with parsley. Serve immediately in mugs or refrigerate 3 hours and serve cold. Makes 8 servings.

Mac & Mo to Go

One teaspoon of oil added to each quart of cooking water will keep macaroni from sticking.

Blue Cheese Dressing, see below
1 small cucumber
8 oz. elbow or salad macaroni, cooked,
  drained, cooled
1 lb. mozzarella cheese, cut in small cubes
1 cup diced celery
1/2 cup diced green pepper

1 cup shredded carrots
1/2 cup watercress leaves
1/2 cup sliced stuffed olives
3/4 cup sliced green onions with tops
8 cherry tomatoes, halved
Watercress sprigs

Blue Cheese Dressing:
1/2 cup mayonnaise
1/2 cup plain yogurt
1/2 cup crumbled blue cheese (2 oz.)
1 tablespoon lemon juice

1/2 teaspoon garlic juice
1 teaspoon sugar
1/2 teaspoon salt

Prepare Blue Cheese Dressing; set aside. Cut unpeeled cucumber in half lengthwise. Scrape out seeds with a spoon. Discard seeds; chop cucumber. In a large bowl, combine chopped cucumber, macaroni, cheese cubes, celery, green pepper, carrots, watercress leaves, olives and green onions with tops. Pour dressing over macaroni mixture. Toss to combine. Refrigerate at least 3 hours. Garnish with cherry tomato halves and watercress sprigs. Makes 10 servings.

Blue Cheese Dressing:
Combine all ingredients in a medium bowl. Beat with a fork until blended.

Cheese & Rice Salad

Because seeds are bitter, they are often removed from salad tomatoes.

1-1/2 cups white rice, uncooked
Water
2 large tomatoes
4 oz. Bel Paese cheese, cut in small cubes
2 oz. fontina cheese, cut in small cubes
1 (4-oz.) can sliced ripe olives, drained
1 tablespoon drained capers

1 (9-oz.) pkg. frozen artichoke hearts,
   cooked, drained, cooled
3 anchovy fillets, chopped
6 tablespoons olive oil
2 tablespoons lemon juice
Watercress sprigs

Cook rice in water according to package directions. Cool to room temperature. Place tomatoes in boiling water 30 seconds to loosen skins. Peel tomatoes and cut each into 4 wedges. Remove seeds with a spoon. Chop seeded peeled tomatoes. In a large bowl, combine cooked rice, chopped tomatoes, Bel Paese and fontina cheese cubes, olives, capers and artichoke hearts. Toss lightly to combine. In a small container with a tight-fitting lid, combine chopped anchovy fillets, olive oil and lemon juice. Shake to blend. Pour over rice mixture. Toss lightly to distribute dressing. Mound on a platter. Garnish with watercress sprigs. Serve at room temperature. Makes 6 servings.

Variation

For a hearty whole-meal dish, surround the mounded rice salad with about 1 cup drained white-meat tuna.

Austrian Potato Salad

Potatoes absorb dressing better when they are hot.

Water
1 teaspoon salt
5 lbs. whole red-skinned potatoes
8 round red radishes
Ice water
1 (8-oz.) jar Italian salad dressing
1 teaspoon dried marjoram leaves, crumbled

1 cup finely chopped onions
1 cup diced celery
1 (3-1/2-oz.) jar capers, drained
1/2 lb. Swiss cheese, diced (2 cups)
Salt and pepper to taste
8 green onions, 3 inches long

Pour water 1 inch deep into a large pot. Bring to a boil. Add 1 teaspoon salt and potatoes. Cover and cook until potatoes are tender when pierced with a fork, 35 to 40 minutes. Drain; set aside. Cut off radish stems and roots. Beginning at top of radishes, cut 4 thin slices of peel almost to the bottom, making 4 petals. Place in a medium bowl. Cover with ice water; set aside. Peel and slice potatoes. Place in a large bowl. Pour dressing over hot sliced potatoes. Cool to room temperature. Add marjoram, onions, celery, capers, diced cheese and salt and pepper to taste. Toss gently to combine. Garnish with radish roses and green onions. Serve immediately or refrigerate. If refrigerated, let stand at room temperature 30 minutes before serving. Makes 6 servings.

Tivoli Gardens Salad

Samsø cheese looks like Swiss, but has a stronger nutty flavor. Tybo is milder.

1 lb. samsø or tybo cheese
1-1/2 cups cubed cooked ham
1/2 cup dairy sour cream
2 tablespoons mayonnaise
2 tablespoons heavy cream or whipping cream
1 tablespoon lemon juice
2 teaspoons snipped fresh chives

1 teaspoon cider vinegar
1 teaspoon Dijon-style mustard
1/8 teaspoon paprika
1 (16-oz.) can sliced beets, drained
1/2 cup chopped sweet pickle
8 small whole sweet pickles

Cube 1/3 of the cheese. Cut remaining cheese into 8 slices. In a medium bowl, toss cubed cheese and ham; set aside. In a small bowl, beat sour cream, mayonnaise, heavy cream or whipping cream, lemon juice, chives, vinegar, mustard and paprika. Add to cubed cheese and ham. Toss to combine. Cut 3/4 cup beet slices into halves. Fold halves into salad with chopped sweet pickle. Spoon salad into a shallow serving bowl. To make pickle fans, cut each pickle into thin lengthwise slices starting just below the stem end. Leave attached at the stem. Spread slices gently apart. Garnish salad with pickle fans, remaining beet slices and cheese slices. Serve at room temperature. Makes 4 to 5 servings.

How to Make Pickle Fans for Tivoli Gardens Salad

1/To make pickle fans, insert knife close to stem end. Cut into thin lengthwise slices.

2/Spread open pickle fans and use with beet slices and cheese slices to garnish salad.

Hot Shrimp-Cheese Salad

You'll love this delicious blend of shrimp, cheese and crisp vegetables.

2 (7-1/2-oz.) cans cooked shrimp, drained,
   chopped
1/2 lb. brick cheese, diced
1 cup chopped celery
1/4 cup chopped toasted almonds
1/4 cup chopped green pepper
1 cup dairy sour cream

1/4 cup crumbled blue cheese (1 oz.)
2 tablespoons minced onion
2 tablespoons lemon juice
1 teaspoon salt
1/2 cup cornflake crumbs
2 tablespoons butter or margarine, melted
1 small lemon, cut in 6 wedges

Preheat oven to 300°F (150°C). Lightly butter six 10-ounce ramekins or ovenproof baking shells. In a large bowl, combine shrimp, diced brick cheese, celery, almonds and green pepper. In a small bowl, blend sour cream, blue cheese, onion, lemon juice and salt with a fork. Add to shrimp mixture, stirring gently. Spoon about 1 cup of the mixture into each prepared ramekin or shell. In a small bowl, stir cornflake crumbs and butter or margarine until crumbs are coated. Sprinkle evenly over each salad. Bake 10 to 15 minutes in preheated oven until heated through. Garnish each serving with a lemon wedge. Serve immediately. Makes 6 servings.

Fruited Orange Crown

To make this mold with flavored gelatin, reduce the water by 1/4 cup and omit the sugar.

1 tablespoon unflavored gelatin powder
2 tablespoons sugar
1/4 teaspoon ground nutmeg
1/8 teaspoon salt
3/4 cup cold water
2 tablespoons undiluted frozen orange juice
   concentrate, thawed

1 (16-oz.) can pineapple chunks, juice pack
1 (16-oz.) can pear halves, juice pack
1 (8-oz.) pkg. cream cheese,
   room temperature
1/2 cup coarsely chopped walnuts

Combine gelatine, sugar, nutmeg and salt in a small saucepan. Stir in water; let stand 5 minutes. Stir in orange juice concentrate. Stir constantly over low heat until gelatin is completely dissolved. Drain juice from pineapple into a 1-cup measure. If necessary, add juice from pears to make 1 cup. Stir into gelatin mixture. Drain pears, saving liquid for another use. Lightly oil a 5- or 6-cup ring mold. Pour gelatin mixture about 1/4 inch deep into mold. Reserve remaining gelatin mixture. Cut 4 of the pear halves in half lengthwise. Place pear pieces in mold, rounded-side down, spacing evenly. Refrigerate mold and reserved gelatin mixture 20 to 40 minutes until gelatin has the consistency of unbeaten egg whites. In a large bowl, beat cream cheese with electric mixer on low speed until smooth and creamy. Gradually beat in reserved gelatin mixture. Beat vigorously 2 minutes with mixer on high speed. Cut remaining pear halves into chunks. Arrange pear chunks and pineapple chunks evenly over partially set gelatin in ring mold. Sprinkle evenly with chopped walnuts. Spoon cream cheese mixture over walnuts and fruit chunks. Refrigerate at least 4 hours. Run a thin knife around edge of mold. Dip bottom of mold briefly into hot water. Place a round platter over mold; invert. Shake gently and remove mold. Makes 6 to 8 servings.

Emmentaler Salad

Emmentaler *is the original Swiss cheese—slightly mild and absolutely delicious.*

2/3 cup mayonnaise
1 teaspoon white wine vinegar
1/4 teaspoon pepper
1/4 teaspoon ground nutmeg

1 lb. Swiss cheese, cut in 1/4-inch cubes
3 tablespoons snipped fresh chives
Boston lettuce leaves

Combine mayonnaise, vinegar, pepper and nutmeg in a small bowl. In a large bowl, toss cheese cubes and chives. Toss again with just enough of the mayonnaise mixture to moisten. Place lettuce leaves on 6 salad plates. Mound cheese mixture on lettuce leaves. Makes 6 servings.

Croque Monsieur

Prepare these French-toasted cheese sandwiches ahead and cook them at the table.

4 slices cooked ham
4 slices Swiss cheese
8 slices firm white bread, crusts removed
1/4 cup butter or margarine

1 teaspoon vegetable oil
4 eggs, slightly beaten
4 tablespoons milk
4 tablespoons currant jelly

Place 1 slice of ham and 1 slice of cheese between 2 slices of bread. Make 3 more sandwiches; set aside. Place butter or margarine and oil in a large skillet over medium heat. Beat eggs and milk in a medium bowl. Moisten edges of each sandwich in egg mixture. Press edges together. Dip both sides of sandwiches in remaining egg mixture. Fry in skillet until golden brown on both sides, turning once. Add more butter or margarine if needed. Top each sandwich with 1 tablespoon currant jelly. Serve immediately. Makes 4 servings.

Variations

Deep-Fried Croque Monsieur: Pour oil for frying 2-1/2 to 3 inches deep in a deep-fryer. Heat to 375°F (190°C). At this temperature a 1-inch cube of bread will turn golden brown in 40 seconds. Cook sandwiches until golden brown on both sides, turning once.

Croque Monte Cristo: Add 4 slices cooked chicken. Garnish each sandwich with 1 tablespoon chutney.

Croque Madame: Substitute 4 large slices cooked turkey breast and 4 slices Gruyère cheese for the ham and Swiss cheese. Substitute raspberry preserves for the currant jelly.

One envelope or 1 tablespoon unflavored gelatin powder will thicken 2 cups of liquid.

Mozzarella in Carozza

Salty anchovies garnish these French-toasted carozzas or envelopes.

4 thick slices mozzarella cheese
8 slices firm white bread, crusts removed
1/4 cup butter or margarine
1 teaspoon vegetable oil

4 eggs, slightly beaten
4 tablespoons milk
16 anchovy fillets
2 tablespoons drained capers

Place 1 slice of cheese between 2 slices of bread. Repeat, making 4 sandwiches; set aside. Place butter or margarine and oil in a large skillet over medium heat. Beat eggs and milk in a medium bowl. Dip sandwich edges in egg mixture; press together. Dip both sides of sandwiches in remaining egg mixture. Fry in skillet until golden brown on both sides, turning once. Add more butter or margarine if needed. To serve, place 4 anchovy fillets around edges and 1 teaspoon capers on center top of each sandwich. Makes 4 servings.

How to Make Croque Monsieur & Other French Toasted Sandwiches

1/Moisten edges of sandwich in egg mixture. Press edges together. Use wooden picks to hold if needed.

2/Dip both sides of sandwiches in egg mixture. Fry in butter or margarine until golden brown.

Sprouts & Feta Pockets

Pita bread is hollow. Cut it in half to make two pockets.

1 tablespoon sesame seeds.	1/4 teaspoon pepper
1 small cucumber	1/2 cup crumbled feta cheese (2 oz.)
2 cups alfalfa sprouts	2 whole-wheat pita breads, cut in half
1/4 cup plain yogurt	1 medium tomato, cut in 4 slices
1/2 teaspoon salt	2 tablespoons snipped fresh mint leaves

Toast sesame seeds in a small skillet over low heat until golden brown, stirring occasionally; set aside. Cut unpeeled cucumber in half lengthwise. Use a spoon to remove seeds. Discard seeds. Chop cucumber; set aside. In a medium bowl, combine sprouts, yogurt, salt, pepper and toasted sesame seeds. Gently stir in feta cheese. Spoon mixture equally into pita bread pockets. Tuck 1 tomato slice into the filling in each pocket. Top with chopped cucumber. Sprinkle with mint leaves. Makes 4 servings.

Varitions

Add sliced ripe olives or chopped green pepper with the cucumbers.

Substitute shredded carrot or thinly sliced celery for the cucumber.

For a milder flavor, substitute cottage cheese for the feta cheese.

Roties à l'Orange

If the edges aren't tightly sealed on these roties or sandwiches, *the filling will leak.*

18 slices firm white bread, crusts removed	Oil for deep-frying
6 tablespoons orange marmalade	4 eggs
3 (3-oz.) pkgs. cream cheese,	4 tablespoons milk
room temperature	Powdered sugar

To make triple-decker sandwiches, spread 6 bread slices with marmalade. Top with 6 more bread slices. Spread with cream cheese. Top with final 6 bread slices. Cut sandwiches in half; set aside. Pour oil 3-1/2 to 4 inches deep in a deep-fryer or a 6-quart kettle with a candy thermometer attached to the side. Heat oil to 375°F (190°C). At this temperature a 1-inch cube of bread will turn golden brown in 40 seconds. Beat eggs and milk in a medium bowl. Dip sandwich halves in egg mixture, holding edges tightly together until saturated. Gently press edges to make a good seal. If edges do not seal, fasten with wooden food picks. With a slotted spoon, lower 1 sandwich at a time into hot oil. Fry until golden brown, turning once. Drain on paper towels. To serve, sprinkle with powdered sugar. Makes 4 to 6 servings.

Fat or oil used for deep-frying may be cooled, strained and refrigerated for reuse unless fish or another strong flavored food was fried in it.

Gouda Grillers

Canadian-style bacon is meaty with very little fat and has a delicious smoked flavor.

1/2 lb. sliced Canadian bacon
1/2 cup orange marmalade
1/4 cup prepared mustard
4 slices pumpernickel bread

2 tablespoons butter or margarine,
   room temperature
1/2 lb. Gouda cheese, cut in 8 slices

Cook bacon in a heavy skillet over low heat until hot, about 3 minutes on each side. Combine marmalade and mustard in a 1-cup measure. Pour over bacon. Simmer 10 minutes, turning bacon often. Preheat broiler. Place bread slices on a baking sheet. Spread butter or margarine evenly on 1 side of bread slices. Top with bacon slices. Spoon 1 teaspoon marmalade glaze over each piece of bacon. Top with cheese slices. Broil sandwiches 3 inches from heat until cheese melts, about 3 minutes. Serve immediately with the remaining glaze. Makes 4 servings.

Variation

Substitute sliced baked ham for the bacon. Put directly into marmalade-mustard mixture just long enough to glaze and heat through.

How to Make Gouda Grillers

1/Top bread slices with bacon rounds that have been sautéed in marmalade mixture.

2/Place cheese slices over sautéed ham and marmalade before broiling.

Savory Ham Bundles

This sandwich is hot from the broiler, so protect your hands and the table.

18 fresh asparagus spears, cooked, drained
6 thin slices cooked ham
1 (8-oz.) pkg. cream cheese, cubed
1/2 cup milk
1 tablespoon dry sherry
1/2 teaspoon onion powder

1/8 teaspoon ground nutmeg
3 slices white bread, toasted
1-1/2 tablespoons butter or margarine,
 room temperature
2 tablespoons grated Parmesan cheese

Place 3 asparagus spears at one end of each slice of ham. Roll up and set aside. In a small saucepan over low heat, combine cream cheese and milk. Stir until cheese melts and mixture is smooth. Stir in sherry, onion powder and nutmeg; keep warm. Preheat broiler. Spread toast slices with butter or margarine; cut diagonally. Place 2 triangles of toast on each of 3 ovenproof plates. Place 1 ham bundle on each piece of toast. Top with 2 tablespoons cream cheese sauce and 1 teaspoon Parmesan cheese. Pour remaining cream cheese sauce into a small serving bowl; set aside. Place plates under broiler. Broil bundles 4 inches from heat until sauce bubbles and Parmesan cheese is golden. Serve immediately with remaining cream cheese sauce. Makes 3 servings.

Variation

Place ham bundles on top of toast triangles in an 8" x 8" baking dish. Top with cream cheese sauce and Parmesan cheese. Broil as directed.

No-Bread Sandwiches

You'll need forks to eat these—they are not finger foods.

Egg Salad Filling, see below
8 large slices Muenster cheese
4 thin slices tomato
4 Boston lettuce leaves

Salt and pepper to taste
Dill pickle wedges
Stuffed olives

Egg Salad Filling:
3 hard-cooked eggs peeled, chopped
1/3 cup minced celery

2 or 3 drops hot pepper sauce
Mayonnaise or salad dressing to moisten

Prepare Egg Salad Filling. Refrigerate 1 hour to blend flavors. Spread 4 cheese slices with filling. Place tomato slices on top of filling. Top with lettuce leaves. Salt and pepper to taste. Cover with remaining cheese slices. Serve on individual plates with pickles and olives. Makes 4 servings.

Egg Salad Filling:
In a small bowl, combine all ingredients, using only enough mayonnaise or salad dressing to moisten.

Corsican Supper Loaf *Photo on page 46.*

Italian bread is similar to French bread but has no sugar in it.

1 large uncut loaf Italian bread or
  French bread
1/4 cup butter or margarine, melted
1/4 teaspoon dried basil leaves, crumbled

1 lb. mozzarella cheese, cut in 8 slices
8 tomato slices, 1/4-inch thick
8 thin slices mild onion

Make 15 cuts in the bread, making 16 equal slices. Do not cut all the way through bottom crust. Combine butter or margarine and basil in a small bowl. Spread on all cut surfaces of bread. Preheat oven to 350°F (175°C). Place sliced loaf on an ungreased baking sheet. In first cut, place 1 slice of cheese, 1 slice of tomato and 1 slice of onion. Place nothing in second cut. Place 1 slice of cheese, tomato and onion in third cut. Repeat until all ingredients are used. Bake 20 to 25 minutes in preheated oven until bread is hot and cheese is melted. To serve, cut through bottom crust at unfilled cuts. Serve immediately. Makes 8 servings.

Variation

Substitute any Cheddar-type cheese, such as Colby, Herkimer, Tillamook, Longhorn or Monterey Jack for the mozzarella cheese.

Grilled Beef & Blue

Serve these outstanding sandwiches with sherry-laced bouillon and a big green salad.

3 tablespoons butter or margarine,
  room temperature
1 tablespoon Dijon-style mustard
3 large crescent rolls, cut in half
  lengthwise
3 large slices rare roast beef

1 egg white
1/4 cup crumbled blue cheese (1 oz.)
1/4 cup shredded brick cheese (1 oz.)
1 green onion, thinly sliced
1 tablespoon grated Romano cheese

Cream butter or margarine and mustard in a small bowl; spread on cut sides of crescent rolls. Place bottom portions of crescent rolls on a broiler pan. Loosely roll beef slices and place on bottom halves of crescent rolls; set aside. In a small bowl, beat egg white with mixer on high speed until stiff peaks form. Fold blue cheese, brick cheese and green onion into beaten egg white. Preheat broiler. Lightly spread egg white mixture over beef rolls. Broil 4 inches from heat until topping is golden and bubbly, about 2 minutes. Place crescent roll tops over egg white mixture. Sprinkle evenly with Romano cheese. Broil 1 minute longer. Serve immediately. Makes 3 servings.

Any vegetable oil except olive oil is acceptable for deep-frying. Olive oil has a strong flavor.

Main Dishes

When planning a menu, your thoughts are likely to turn first to protein-rich meat, fish, poultry or eggs. But cheese belongs on that list too. Cheese is also rich in protein and very satisfying. There are so many kinds of cheeses, textures and flavors that it's difficult to find anyone who doesn't enjoy at least one kind of cheese.

Generally, a cheese main dish is less expensive than a meat, fish or poultry dish, so it's a welcome budget stretcher. Most cheese main dishes include a sauce, vegetables and an extender such as rice, noodles, macaroni or bread. Cheeses that have ripened three months or longer will melt into sauces or casseroles better than fresh cheeses. *Colby* and *Longhorn*, both Cheddar cheeses, are aged and have slightly higher moisture content than other Cheddars. This makes them two of the best cooking cheeses available. Another excellent melting and blending cheese is *pasteurized process* cheese.

Some of the sharper flavored cheeses like *Swiss* or sharp Cheddar are especially good in dressings or stuffings where they enhance somewhat bland flavors. In Pork Loin Alpine-Style, a savory *Gruyère* cheese stuffing is spooned into pockets cut in a pork loin roast. Ask your butcher to crack the backbone, then you can easily make cuts in the meat between the cracks for stuffing. It will look as if you worked for hours when, in fact, you will have the stuffed roast in the oven in about 15 minutes. Gruyère is a Swiss cheese.

In two recipes, Chicken Monterey and Turkey Cutlets Norwegian-Style, you will need to pound the meat to break down the tissue. Place the meat between two pieces of waxed paper and beat it with a heavy object such as a wooden or metal meat mallet. This tenderizes and flattens the meat. If the meat is coated with flour, the flour is beaten into the meat for richer flavor and easier browning. If you don't have a meat mallet, use the edge of a heavy thick saucer—plastic is best. Don't use thin china because it will break.

Easy on the Budget Supper
Lasagna Verde, page 67
Easy Breadsticks, page 37
Lettuce Wedges with Italian Dressing
Raspberry Sherbet
Coconut Macaroons

Deviled Eggs Indienne

Add cooked vegetables at the last minute to keep from crushing them as foods are combined.

2 cups long-grain white rice, uncooked	1 cup boiling water
Water	1/4 cup butter or margarine
8 hard-cooked eggs, peeled	1 medium onion, chopped
1/4 cup mayonnaise	1/4 cup all-purpose flour
1/2 teaspoon salt	1/2 teaspoon salt
1/2 teaspoon dry mustard	1/8 teaspoon white pepper
1/8 teaspoon white pepper	1-1/2 teaspoons curry powder
2 teaspoons finely chopped canned pimiento	1/4 teaspoon ground ginger
1-1/2 cups shredded Swiss cheese (6 oz.)	1 cup milk
1 teaspoon instant chicken broth granules	1 (10-oz.) pkg. frozen peas, cooked, drained

Cook rice in water according to package directions; set aside and keep hot. Halve eggs lengthwise; remove yolks. In a small bowl, blend mayonnaise, 1/2 teaspoon salt, dry mustard, 1/8 teaspoon white pepper, pimiento and 1/4 cup of the cheese. Press egg yolks through a sieve into mayonnaise mixture. Stir gently until combined. Spoon yolk mixture into egg white halves; set aside. Dissolve chicken broth granules in boiling water. Set aside to cool. Melt butter or margarine in a medium saucepan over low heat. Add onion; sauté until tender but not browned, about 5 minutes. Stir in flour, 1/2 teaspoon salt, 1/8 teaspoon white pepper, curry powder and ginger. Cook and stir over medium heat until mixture bubbles. Stir cooled broth and milk into onion mixture. Continue to stir until sauce bubbles and thickens. Remove from heat and stir in remaining cheese until melted. Gently stir in peas. Spoon hot cooked rice into a warm shallow serving dish; spoon sauce over rice. Arrange stuffed egg halves around edge of dish. Serve immediately. Makes 4 to 6 servings.

Turkish-Style Lamb Patties

For a more authentic flavor, substitute feta cheese for the cream cheese.

3 green onions with some tops, thinly sliced	1/4 teaspoon dried oregano leaves, crumbled
1-1/2 lbs. lean ground lamb	3 garlic cloves, pressed
1/2 lb. lean ground beef	1/2 lb. Gruyère cheese, cut in 6 slices
1 tablespoon dried parsley leaves	1 (3-oz.) pkg. cream cheese, room temperature
2 teaspoons salt	
1/2 teaspoon pepper	1/2 cup plain yogurt
1/4 teaspoon ground cumin	2 tablespoons snipped fresh mint leaves

In a medium bowl, combine green onions, lamb, beef, parsley, salt, pepper, cumin, oregano and garlic. Divide into 12 equal portions. Shape each portion into a thin, flat patty. Preheat broiler if required. Place cheese slices on top of 6 patties; trim so cheese is slightly smaller than patty. Top with remaining patties. Carefully pinch edges to seal cheese inside. Broil 2 to 3 inches from source of heat, turning once. Broil about 3 minutes, on each side for medium rare. While patties broil, beat cream cheese and yogurt in a small bowl until fluffy. Just before serving, place 1 teaspoonful of the yogurt mixture on top of each patty. Sprinkle with mint leaves for garnish. Makes 6 servings.

Marissa's Cress & Cheese Manicotti

Use an iced-tea spoon to fill manicotti with the peppery watercress mixture.

1 (12-oz.) pkg. manicotti shells
Water
2 cups cream-style cottage cheese (1 lb.)
1 (8-oz.) pkg. cream cheese, room temperature
1 cup finely snipped watercress leaves,
  without stems
2 eggs, slightly beaten
1 teaspoon salt
1/2 teaspoon onion powder
6 tablespoons butter or margarine

6 tablespoons all-purpose flour
1 teaspoon dry mustard
1 teaspoon salt
4 cups milk
4 cups shredded Muenster cheese (1 lb.)
3/4 cup fine dry breadcrumbs, page 108
1/4 cup freshly grated Romano cheese
  (3/4 oz.)
1 tablespoon sweet paprika

Cook manicotti in water according to package directions. Drain and rinse; drain again. Cover with ice water. Preheat oven to 350°F (175°C). In a medium bowl, combine cottage cheese, cream cheese, watercress, eggs, 1 teaspoon salt and onion powder; set aside. Melt butter or margarine in a medium saucepan. Stir in flour, dry mustard and 1 teaspoon salt. Cook until mixture bubbles, stirring constantly. Gradually stir in milk; continue stirring until sauce bubbles and thickens. Remove from heat and stir in Muenster cheese until melted. Spoon about 1/3 of the sauce into an ungreased 13" x 9" baking dish. Drain manicotti on paper towels. Fill with cottage cheese mixture. Place in rows in a single layer in baking dish. Spoon remaining sauce over and around manicotti. Combine breadcrumbs, Romano cheese and paprika in a small bowl; sprinkle over casserole. Bake about 1 hour in preheated oven until heated through and bubbling. Makes 8 servings.

Rosa's Fettuccini Verde

Green noodles are usually made from spinach pasta and are absolutely delicious.

1 (12-oz.) pkg. green fettuccini
Water
1/2 cup butter or margarine
1/2 cup heavy cream or whipping cream
1 teaspoon grated onion
2 egg yolks

3/4 cup shredded mozzarella cheese (3 oz.)
1/2 cup freshly grated Parmesan cheese
  (1-1/2 oz.)
1-1/2 cups shredded prosciutto ham
  (about 1/2 lb.)

Cook fettuccini in water according to package directions until tender but still firm. Drain well and set aside. Melt butter in a large saucepan over medium-low heat. Do not remove from heat. Vigorously stir in cream, onion and egg yolks until well blended and hot but not boiling. Stir in cheeses until melted. Add drained fettuccini. Toss to coat each strand with cheese sauce. Spoon into a warm shallow serving dish and sprinkle with prosciutto ham. Serve immediately. Makes 6 servings.

Variation

If prosciutto is not available, substitute other dry, strong-flavored ham such as Westphalian or Southern country-style.

Gouda Piccata

Refrigerating the cheese slices sets the coating and keeps the cheese from melting into the pan.

1 cup all-purpose flour
2 cups cornflake crumbs
2 eggs
6 large slices cold Gouda cheese, 1/2-inch thick
1/4 cup butter or margarine
1/4 cup vegetable oil
Juice of 1 lemon (2 to 3 tablespoons)

Grated peel of 1 lemon
  (about 1-1/2 teaspoons)
2 tablespoons hot water
2 tablespoons drained capers, if desired
Lemon twists
Parsley sprigs

Line a large baking sheet with waxed paper; set aside. Place flour and cornflake crumbs in separate dishes. Beat eggs in a pie plate or other shallow dish until blended. Remove cheese slices from refrigerator. Working quickly, dip each slice into flour, into eggs, and into cornflake crumbs. Be sure cheese is completely covered at each step. Place coated cheese slices on prepared baking sheet. Slices should not touch one another. Refrigerate 1-1/2 hours. Heat butter and oil in a large skillet. Add cheese slices 2 or 3 at a time. Skillet should not be crowded. Brown 1 to 2 minutes on each side, turning only once with a broad spatula. Place cooked cheese slices on a heated serving platter; keep warm. Discard all but 2 tablespoons drippings from skillet. Add lemon juice, lemon peel and hot water to skillet. Bring to a boil, stirring to loosen browned bits. Pour over cheese slices. If desired, sprinkle with capers. Garnish with lemon twists and parsley sprigs. Serve immediately. Makes 6 servings.

How to Make Gouda Piccata

1/Dip each cheese slice into flour, eggs and cornflake crumbs, coating thoroughly each time.

2/Pour lemon sauce over cheese slices. Garnish with lemon twists and parsley sprigs.

Lasagna Verde

Colorful and nutritious green pastas are usually made from spinach, semolina flour, eggs and salt.

12 green lasagna noodles
Water
1-1/2 lbs. fresh spinach, washed, trimmed
2 tablespoons water
1/4 cup butter or margarine
1 medium onion, chopped
1 garlic clove, pressed
1/4 cup all-purpose flour
1 (15-oz.) can chicken broth
1 (8-oz.) can tomato sauce

1 cup dairy sour cream
3/4 teaspoon dried thyme leaves, crumbled
1/8 teaspoon ground nutmeg
Salt and white pepper to taste
2 cups ricotta cheese (1 lb.)
1 cup shredded Monterey Jack cheese (4 oz.)
1 cup freshly grated Romano cheese (3 oz.)
3/4 cup fine dry breadcrumbs, page 108
Paprika

Cook lasagna noodles in water according to package directions. Drain and rinse in cold water to prevent sticking; set aside. In a large saucepan, cook spinach about 3 minutes in 2 tablespoons water. Drain and set aside. Preheat oven to 350°F (175°C). Very lightly oil a 13" x 9" baking dish; set aside. Melt butter or margarine in a medium saucepan. Add onion and garlic; sauté until tender but not browned. Stir in flour until mixture bubbles. Gradually stir in chicken broth and tomato sauce. Stir constantly over medium heat until mixture bubbles and thickens. Lower heat and stir in sour cream, thyme, nutmeg and salt and white pepper to taste; do not boil. Place 6 of the cooked noodles on bottom of prepared baking dish. Layer cooked spinach, ricotta cheese and Monterey Jack cheese evenly over noodles. Top with 1/2 of the sauce. Cover with remaining 6 noodles and remaining sauce. In a small bowl, combine Romano cheese and breadcrumbs; sprinkle over lasagna. Garnish with paprika. Bake 20 to 25 minutes in preheated oven until lasagna is heated through and cheese is melted. Let stand 5 minutes; cut into squares. Makes 6 servings.

Little Beef & Blue Loaves

Semisoft blue cheese is used extensively in cooking, salads and salad dressing.

2 lbs. lean ground beef
1 (1-lb.) can tomatoes, well-drained
1 cup soft breadcrumbs, page 108
1 egg, slightly beaten

1-1/2 teaspoons salt
1/4 teaspoon pepper
1 teaspoon Worcestershire sauce
3/4 cup crumbled blue cheese (3 oz.)

Preheat oven to 350°F (175°C). In a medium bowl, combine beef, tomatoes, breadcrumbs, egg, salt, pepper and Worcestershire sauce. Mix well, breaking up tomatoes if necessary. Divide meat mixture into 12 portions. On a baking sheet with raised edges, shape 6 portions into rectangles 1/2-inch thick. Sprinkle 1 tablespoon of the cheese over each rectangle. Cover with remaining 6 portions shaping and pinching to seal cheese between meat. With the back of a spoon, make a shallow depression in the top of each loaf. Bake 30 minutes in preheated oven. Spoon remaining cheese equally in depressions on top of loaves. Bake 10 minutes longer until cheese is soft and meat well-browned. If freezing cooked loaves, do not place cheese in depressions on top of loaves. Wrap loaves separately; label, date and freeze. To reheat, place frozen meat loaves in 350°F (175°C) oven. Bake 1 hour. Spoon remaining cheese into depressions and bake 15 minutes longer. Makes 6 servings.

Classic Cheese Soufflé

Make a groove around the edge so the top rises and forms the classic top hat as the soufflé cooks.

1/3 cup butter or margarine	1-1/2 cups milk
1/3 cup all-purpose flour	2 cups shredded sharp Cheddar cheese (8 oz.)
1 teaspoon salt	6 eggs, separated
1/8 teaspoon cayenne pepper	

Melt butter or margarine in a medium saucepan over low heat. Stirring constantly, add flour, salt and cayenne pepper. Cook until mixture bubbles. Add milk gradually, stirring constantly. Stir and cook until mixture bubbles and thickens. Stir in cheese until melted. Remove cheese mixture from heat. Beat egg yolks slightly until combined. Gradually stir 1/3 cup hot cheese mixture into egg yolks. Stir egg yolk mixture into remaining cheese mixture. Cool 10 minutes. Preheat oven to 300°F (150°C). In a medium bowl, beat egg whites until stiff but not dry. Fold cooled cheese mixture into egg whites. Spoon mixture into a 2-quart soufflé dish or casserole with straight sides. With the tip of a spoon, make a shallow groove 1 inch from edge around top of soufflé. Bake 1 hour 15 minutes in preheated oven until center has risen about 1-1/2 inches above groove and turned golden brown. Serve immediately. Makes 6 servings.

How to Make Pork Loin Alpine-Style

1/Use a sharp knife to cut deep pockets over, not between, rib bones.

Pork Loin Alpine-Style

Fresh sauerkraut from your supermarket's refrigerated section is milder than canned sauerkraut.

2 cups chopped green peppers
1/3 cup chopped onion
1/4 cup butter or margarine
3 cups herb-flavored stuffing mix
2 tablespoons dried parsley leaves
1 teaspoon salt
1/4 teaspoon black pepper

1 (1-lb.) can whole tomatoes, undrained
12 oz. Gruyère cheese, finely diced
1 (5- to 7-lb.) pork loin,
    with backbone cracked
2 lbs. fresh or canned sauerkraut
1 tablespoon caraway seeds, if desired

Place green peppers and onion in a cold skillet; add butter or margarine. Cook over medium heat, stirring often, until vegetables are golden. Stir in stuffing mix, parsley, salt, pepper, tomatoes and 2 cups of the cheese; remove from heat. Preheat oven to 325°F (165°C). With a sharp knife, cut 6 to 10 deep pockets over each rib bone. Fill pockets with stuffing mixture. Place any leftover stuffing in a lightly greased baking dish and bake with roast during last half hour of roasting time. Insert meat thermometer in thickest part of meat, not touching bone. Place roast on a rack in a shallow roasting pan with pocket openings up. Cook 35 minutes per pound in preheated oven or until meat thermometer registers 170°F (75°C). Place sauerkraut in a sieve and rinse under running hot water; set aside to drain. Use a bulb baster or spoon to remove 1/4 cup pork drippings from roasting pan 1/2 hour before end of cooking time. Heat drippings in a heavy skillet until sizzling. Add rinsed sauerkraut and caraway seeds, if desired. Cook over medium heat until hot and lightly browned, turning often with a fork. Keep warm over low heat until roast is done. Spread sauerkraut on a warm platter and sprinkle with remaining cheese. Place roast on top of sauerkraut. Carve by slicing between rib bones. Makes 8 to 10 servings.

2/Fill pockets with cheese stuffing. Bake excess stuffing in a separate dish.

3/Place baked pork loin on a layer of sauerkraut. Slice between rib bones and stuffed pockets.

Turkey Cutlets Norwegian-Style

Dredge *means to coat, usually with flour. It helps with the browning and keeps the juices in.*

8 (1/2-inch) turkey breast cutlets
1/2 cup all-purpose flour
2 tablespoons butter or margarine
1 tablespoon vegetable oil
8 small whole carrots
4 small zucchini, cut in half lengthwise
Water

Salt and pepper to taste
1-1/2 cups dairy sour cream
1 cup shredded gjetost cheese (4 oz.)
1-1/2 tablespoons lemon juice
1/4 teaspoon salt
Pepper to taste

Place turkey cutlets between 2 pieces of waxed paper. Pound with a meat mallet until cutlets are 1/4-inch thick. Dredge pounded cutlets in flour. Heat butter or margarine and oil in a heavy skillet over medium-high heat. Add cutlets; brown lightly on both sides. Reduce heat. Cook until tender and juices run colorless when cutlets are pierced with a fork; keep warm. Cook carrots and zucchini separately in medium saucepans in water 1/2 inch deep until crisp-tender. Set aside; keep warm. Arrange cooked cutlets on a warm platter. Season with salt and pepper; keep warm. Pour drippings from cutlets into skillet as accumulated on platter. With a fork or whisk, stir sour cream into drippings in skillet. Over low heat, stir in cheese until melted; do not boil. Stir in lemon juice, 1/4 teaspoon salt and pepper to taste. Arrange cooked carrots and zucchini around cutlets on platter. Spoon dripping mixture over cutlets and vegetables. Serve immediately. Makes 8 servings.

Classic Welsh Rabbit

Whether you call it rarebit *or* rabbit, *it's easy to make and superb to eat.*

1 cup beer
1 teaspoon dry mustard
2 teaspoons Worcestershire sauce
3 or 4 drops hot pepper sauce

4 cups shredded Cheddar cheese (1 lb.)
2 eggs
1 tablespoon cornstarch
4 English muffins, halved, toasted

Combine beer, mustard, Worcestershire sauce and hot pepper sauce in the top of a double boiler. Place over simmering water and cook until warmed through. Stir in cheese 1 cup at a time until melted. In a small bowl, beat eggs and cornstarch until blended. Gradually stir 1/2 cup hot cheese mixture into egg mixture. Stir egg-cheese mixture into remaining cheese mixture in top of double boiler. Continue to cook and stir over simmering water 3 minutes longer. Place 2 muffin halves on each of 4 dinner plates. Top with cheese mixture. Serve immediately. Makes 4 servings.

Variations

Scotch Woodcock: Place 1 poached egg on each muffin half before spooning on cheese sauce.
Bacon & Tomato Rabbit: Place a 1/4-inch slice of tomato on each muffin half; spoon on cheese sauce. Top with thick-sliced bacon, cooked crisp, drained well.

Chicken Monterey

Pull the bones from the chicken breasts or cut them with a knife.

4 chicken breasts
1/4 cup butter or margarine,
   room temperature
1/2 teaspoon dried oregano leaves, crumbled
1 tablespoon snipped fresh parsley
1/2 cup fine dry breadcrumbs, page 108
1/2 cup freshly grated Parmesan cheese
   (1-1/2 oz.)

1/4 teaspoon garlic powder
1/4 teaspoon salt
1/4 teaspoon pepper
1 teaspoon dried oregano leaves, crumbled
1/4 lb. Monterey Jack cheese
5 tablespoons butter or margarine, melted
1 orange, thinly sliced

Carefully cut bones from chicken breasts and remove skin. Cut breast in half lengthwise. Place each chicken breast half between 2 pieces of waxed paper. Pound with a meat mallet until about 1/4 inch thick; set aside. Combine 1/4 cup butter or margarine, 1/2 teaspoon oregano and parsley in a small bowl; set aside. In a pie plate, stir together breadcrumbs, Parmesan cheese, garlic powder, salt, pepper and 1 teaspoon oregano; set aside. Spread herb-butter mixture evenly over pounded chicken breasts. Cut Monterey Jack cheese into eight 1-1/2" x 1/2" strips. Place 1 cheese strip on each pounded chicken piece. Roll chicken around cheese, tucking ends under. Dip chicken rolls in 5 tablespoons melted butter or margarine. Carefully roll in breadcrumb mixture. Place seam-side down 1/2 inch apart in an ungreased 13" x 9" baking dish. Cover and refrigerate 4 hours or overnight. Preheat oven to 400°F (205°C). Remove chicken rolls from refrigerator. Bake uncovered about 20 minutes in preheated oven until juices no longer run pink when chicken is pierced with a fork. Place chicken rolls on a hot platter. Garnish with orange slices. Makes 8 servings.

One-Pot Wonder

Parmesan is a hard, dry, sharp-flavored Italian cheese. It is marvelous in soups, salads and pastas.

1 egg
1/2 teaspoon ground nutmeg
1-1/4 teaspoons salt
1/4 teaspoon pepper
1 tablespoon dried parsley leaves
1-1/2 lbs. lean ground beef
1/3 cup fine dry breadcrumbs, page 108
6 oz. Swiss cheese, cut in 1/2-inch cubes

2 tablespoons vegetable oil
3 medium onions, chopped
1 (46-oz.) can tomato juice
1 (8-oz.) pkg. medium egg noodles, uncooked
1/2 teaspoon dried thyme leaves, crumbled
1/2 teaspoon sugar
1/4 teaspoon pepper
3/4 cup grated Parmesan cheese (2-1/4 oz.)

Beat egg, nutmeg, salt and 1/4 teaspoon pepper in a large bowl. Stir in parsley, beef and breadcrumbs. Mold about 2 tablespoons beef mixture around each Swiss cheese cube. Heat oil in a 4-quart pot. Brown meatballs 10 or 12 at a time on all sides. Remove meatballs; set aside. Add onions to pot. Cook until softened and very lightly browned. Add tomato juice. Bring to a boil. Add noodles gradually so liquid continues to boil. Stir in browned meatballs, thyme, sugar and 1/4 teaspoon pepper. Cover and reduce heat. Simmer 10 minutes, stirring occasionally. Gently stir in 1/4 cup of the Parmesan cheese. Spoon into a warm serving dish. Sprinkle with remaining Parmesan cheese. Serve immediately. Makes 6 servings.

Pastel de Pollo con Queso

If you prefer, bake the rolls in a well-greased pan in a 400°F (205°C) oven for 20 minutes.

1 broiler-fryer, cut up (about 3 lbs.)
2 (13-3/4-oz.) cans chicken broth
1/2 cup chopped onion
1 cup thinly sliced celery
2 medium carrots, sliced
1/3 cup butter or margarine

1/2 cup all-purpose flour
1 cup heavy cream or whipping cream
1 cup shredded sharp Cheddar or
   fontina cheese (4 oz.)
Salt and pepper to taste
Topper Roll, see below

Topper Roll:
1 (3-oz.) pkg. cream cheese,
   room temperature
2 tablespoons half-and-half or light cream
1 tablespoon snipped fresh parsley

1 tablespoon snipped fresh chives
1/4 teaspoon salt
2 cups biscuit mix
1/2 cup milk

Place chicken pieces in a large pot or Dutch oven. Add broth, onion, celery and carrots. Cover and bring to a boil. Lower heat and simmer about 45 minutes until chicken is tender. With a slotted spoon, remove chicken and vegetables from broth; place in a 2-quart casserole dish. Set aside and keep warm. Melt butter or margarine in a medium saucepan. Add flour. Cook and stir until mixture bubbles. Measure 2 cups broth from pot and slowly stir into flour mixture. Continue stirring until mixture bubbles and thickens. Blend in cream until heated through; do not boil. Stir in cheese until melted. Season sauce with salt and pepper to taste. Keep warm. Preheat oven to 400°F (205°C). Prepare Topper Roll. Pour sauce over chicken and vegetables in casserole. Lay Topper Roll slices flat side-by-side around edge of casserole. Bake 25 minutes in preheated oven until lightly browned. Serve at once. Makes 6 servings.

Topper Roll:
Combine cream cheese and half-and-half or light cream in a small bowl. Beat until fluffy. Gently stir in parsley, chives and salt; set aside. Combine biscuit mix and milk in a medium bowl. Dough will form a ball and leave side of bowl. Turn dough onto a lightly floured surface. Knead several times until mixture forms a smooth ball. Roll dough out to an 8-inch square. Spread cream cheese mixture evenly over dough. Roll up jelly-roll fashion. With a sharp knife, cut into 8 even slices.

Butter used to grease pans becomes too brown if foods are baked at 400°F (205°C) or higher.

Cazuela de Queso y Tortillas

Use garlic juice when you want a mild garlic flavor that blends rather than overpowers.

16 corn tortillas
1 (7-oz.) can whole green chile peppers
2 medium white onions, coarsely chopped
1 cup coarsely chopped walnuts
1 (12-oz.) can pitted ripe olives,
   drained, halved
4 cups shredded Monterey Jack cheese (1 lb.)
4 cups shredded Longhorn cheese (1 lb.)
1/2 cup butter or margarine

2 cups half-and-half or light cream
1 cup dairy sour cream
1-1/2 teaspoons dried oregano leaves, crumbled
1 teaspoon garlic juice
1/2 teaspoon salt
2 canned whole red pimientos,
   cut in thin strips
2 avocados, peeled, sliced

Preheat oven to 300°F (150°C). Generously butter a deep 4-quart casserole dish. Cover bottom with 5 overlapping tortillas; set aside. Remove seeds and membranes from green chiles. Coarsely chop green chiles. Over tortillas, layer 1/2 each of the onions, green chiles, walnuts and olives. Toss Monterey Jack and Longhorn cheeses in a large bowl to combine. Sprinkle 2 cups of the combined cheeses over olives on top of casserole; set aside. Melt butter or margarine in a medium saucepan; cool slightly. Stir in half-and-half or light cream, sour cream, oregano, garlic juice and salt. Stir over low heat until mixture is lukewarm (115°F, 45°C) and blended. Spoon 1 cup of the sauce over cheeses in casserole. Again layer 5 tortillas, remaining 1/2 each of the onions, green chiles, walnuts, olives and 2 cups of the cheeses. Top with remaining 6 tortillas, remaining sauce and 2 cups of the cheeses. Bake 60 to 75 minutes in preheated oven. Increase oven temperature to 400°F (205°C). Remove casserole from oven and sprinkle remaining cheeses over casserole. Arrange pimiento strips and avocado slices on top of cheeses. Bake 5 minutes until cheese softens and pimiento strips and avocado slices begin sinking into softened cheeses. Makes 10 servings.

Flounder Mornay

When fish flakes or is easily pulled apart with two forks, it is ready to serve.

2 (10-oz.) pkgs. frozen broccoli spears
Water
2 lbs. frozen flounder fillets, thawed
1/4 cup butter or margarine
1/4 cup chopped onion
1/4 cup all-purpose flour

3 cups milk
1-1/2 teaspoons salt
1/4 teaspoon white pepper
2 cups shredded Swiss cheese (8 oz.)
1/4 cup snipped fresh parsley

Preheat oven to 350°F (175°C). Lightly butter a shallow 3-quart casserole dish. Cook broccoli spears in water according to package directions; drain. Arrange cooked broccoli in a single layer in prepared casserole dish. Cut fish fillets into serving-size portions. Arrange over broccoli; set aside. Melt butter or margarine in a medium saucepan. Add onion. Sauté until tender but not browned. Stir in flour until mixture bubbles. Add milk; stir constantly until mixture bubbles and thickens. Add salt, white pepper and cheese. Stir until cheese melts. Pour over fish. Bake about 30 minutes in preheated oven until fish flakes easily. Garnish with parsley. Serve immediately. Makes 8 servings.

Savory Pies

The English have long distinguished between *savory* and *sweet* pies. Savory means piquant, pungent, salty or not sweet. Pizza and quiche, the two savory pies in this section, are quite different from one another but both can be defined as a crisp crust with a flavorful filling incorporating lots of cheese. Pizza usually calls for a yeast-raised crust topped with highly seasoned garnishes and generously sprinkled with cheese. Quiche usually has an unsweetened pie crust with a custard filling containing cheese and meat or vegetables.

Pie crust pastry should be tender, flaky and delicately crisp. When baked it is golden brown with a blistered surface. The flavor should be bland and pleasant. Add 1/2 cup shredded cheese to the dry ingredients if you desire, then add four tablespoons more liquid than called for in the basic recipe. See Standard Pastry for Cheese Pies, page 77. Handle pie dough very little to prevent the gluten in the flour from over-developing.

Some recipes instruct you to prepare the crust by *baking blind.* This is a simple procedure where the crust is filled with a liner and rice or beans to keep the crust from pulling away from the sides of the pan while it bakes. You'll find instructions in the box on page 85.

Farmhouse Pizza and Cheese & Vegetable Pie Italian-Style have double crusts and firm fillings. If the filling in a double-crust pie is firm enough to keep the top pastry from sinking into it, the pastry can be rolled out on a lightly floured surface and folded in fourths to make a large wedge. Place the wedge on top of the pie with the point in the center. Unfold the pastry and crimp or flute the edges. If the filling is liquid, fold the pastry in half and lay it over a rolling pin. Lift the top pastry to the pie, placing the edge of the pastry even with the edge of the pan. Gently lower the pastry onto the pie. Slide out the rolling pin and unfold the pastry.

Use some of your basic baking pans to make savory pies. For large pizzas, use baking sheets with raised edges and cut the pizza in squares for serving. Some thick-crust Sicilian-style pizzas are baked in 8-inch or 9-inch square pans. But a round, shallow 12-inch pizza pan is a good investment if you love homemade pizza. Quiche is often baked in 8-inch, 9-inch, or 10-inch pie pans. If you prefer just-right utensils, you'll want to own a quiche pan. Quiche pans are generally shallow with fluted rims and removable bottoms which make it easy to remove the quiche.

Pizza Party
Farmhouse Pizza, page 80
Big Thick-Crust Pizza, page 82
Marinated Mushrooms
Tossed Green Salad
Blue Cheese Cream Dressing, page 45
Lemon Ice Cream

Huntingdonshire Tart

Brushing the pastry with an egg-water mixture gives it a shiny brown crust.

Double Pâte Brisée dough from Holiday
   Main-Dish Cheesecake, page 86
1 egg
1 tablespoon cold water
2 tablespoons minced green onion
2 medium tomatoes, peeled, thinly sliced,
   well drained

3 cups crumbled Stilton cheese (12 oz.)
4 eggs
2 cups heavy cream or whipping cream
3/4 teaspoon salt
1/4 teaspoon pepper
1 cup small fresh parsley sprigs

Preheat oven to 400°F (205°C). Prepare Pâte Brisée dough. Roll out and fit into a 10-inch quiche pan with or without removable bottom. Bake blind 15 minutes; see Baking Blind, page 85. Remove liner and beans or rice. In a small bowl, lightly beat 1 egg with water. Brush inside of baked shell with egg mixture. Bake 2 minutes longer; set aside. Reduce oven temperature to 375°F (190°C). Sprinkle green onions into bottom of cooked pastry shell. Arrange tomato slices over onions; sprinkle with cheese. Lightly beat 4 eggs in a medium bowl. Beat in cream, salt and pepper. Pour over cheese in pastry shell. Bake 35 to 40 minutes in preheated oven until puffed and lightly browned. Garnish with parsley sprigs around edge. Let stand 10 minutes before cutting in wedges. Makes 6 to 8 servings.

Standard Pastry for Cheese Pies

Measure accurately and handle lightly. A pie is only as good as its crust.

Single-Crust 9- or 10-inch pie:
1 cup all-purpose flour
1/2 teaspoon salt
1/3 cup vegetable shortening
3 tablespoons cold water

Double-Crust 9- or 10-inch pie:
2 cups all-purpose flour
1/2 teaspoon salt
3/4 cup vegetable shortening
6 tablespoons water

Sift flour and salt into a medium bowl. With a pastry blender or 2 knives used scissors-fashion, cut in shortening until mixture resembles corn meal. Sprinkle cold water evenly over surface. Stir with a fork until dough clings together and leaves side of bowl. Shape into 1 ball for a single-crust pastry, 2 balls for a double-crust pastry. On a floured surface, roll out 1 ball to a 12-inch circle, using a light rolling motion from center toward outer edge. Turn dough often to prevent sticking. If dough sticks, lift carefully with a spatula and sprinkle a little flour underneath. Fold rolled pastry in half and place lengthwise over rolling pin; lift gently to pie pan, centering fold of pastry before withdrawing rolling pin. Without stretching pastry, press gently into pan. Trim bottom pastry shell even with edge of pan. For double-crust pastry, roll second pastry ball in the same manner. Arrange over filling. Trim top pastry 1/2 inch larger than pan. Fold edge of top pastry under bottom pastry shell and pinch with fingers to form a high-standing edge. For a low, smooth edge, you may cut edges of both pastries even with pan rim and crimp with a fork to seal. To bake a single pastry shell prick bottom and sides thoroughly with a fork and bake at 425°F (220°C) 25 to 30 minutes.

Greek Spinach Pie

Spanakopeta, *as it is known in Greece, depends on ricotta and feta cheeses for its creamy texture.*

Standard Pastry for Cheese Pie,
   Double-Crust, page 77
3 eggs
3 tablespoons butter or margarine
1 cup chopped onions
1 cup ricotta cheese (8 oz.) or
   1 cup Labna, page 17

1 (10-oz.) pkg. frozen chopped spinach,
   thawed, well-drained
1/2 teaspoon salt
1/4 teaspoon pepper
1-1/2 cups crumbled feta cheese (12 oz.)
1 medium tomato, cut in 6 wedges

Prepare pastry. Roll out half of pastry and fit into a 9-inch pie pan; do not prick. Separate 1 egg; place yolk in a large bowl. Stir egg white with a fork and brush over bottom and side of pastry shell. Add leftover egg white to yolk in bowl. Add remaining 2 eggs; set aside. Melt butter or margarine in a medium skillet over low heat. Add onions; sauté until soft but not browned. Preheat oven to 425°F (220°C). Beat eggs until whites and yolks are blended but not frothy. Stir in ricotta or Labna cheese, spinach, salt, pepper and sautéed onions. Gently stir in feta cheese. Pour egg mixture into pastry shell. Roll out and place top crust over filling. Trim and crimp edge with fingers or a fork. Bake 30 minutes in preheated oven until crust is golden and a knife inserted in center comes out clean. Cool on a rack 10 minutes before cutting. Garnish with tomato wedges. Makes 6 to 8 servings.

Scandinavian Cloud

This one has no crust—just an airy filling with an intriguing flavor.

3 tablespoons butter or margarine
2 tablespoons minced green onion
3 drops garlic juice
1-1/2 cups minced cooked ham
1/4 cup Madeira wine
3 eggs, separated
1 cup dairy sour cream

1/4 cup soft white breadcrumbs, page 108
1/2 cup shredded Jarlsberg cheese (2 oz.)
2 teaspoons caraway seeds, if desired
1/2 teaspoon salt
1/8 teaspoon white pepper
1/4 teaspoon cream of tartar

Melt butter or margarine in a medium skillet over medium-low heat. Add green onion, garlic juice and ham. Cook 5 minutes; add wine. Turn heat to high and stir constantly until liquid evaporates, about 5 minutes. Remove from heat and cool 15 minutes. Preheat oven to 400°F (205°C). Generously butter a 9-inch quiche pan or shallow pie pan. In a medium bowl, beat egg yolks until thick and pale. Stir in sour cream, breadcrumbs, cheese and caraway seeds, if desired. Stir in cooled ham mixture. In a large bowl, beat egg whites until foamy. Add salt, white pepper and cream of tartar. Beat until stiff peaks form. Fold egg whites into ham mixture. Spoon into prepared pan. Bake 30 to 35 minutes in preheated oven until puffed and browned. Serve immediately. Makes 4 to 6 servings.

Pizza Pesto

Shortening can be used in the crust, but the flavor and texture will be slightly different.

Parmesan Pizza Crust, see below
2 garlic cloves, minced
1/4 cup freshly grated Parmesan cheese
   (3/4 oz.)
1/2 cup pine nuts, crushed
2 teaspoons dried basil leaves, crumbled
2 tablespoons dried parsley leaves

1/2 teaspoon salt
1/4 teaspoon pepper
2 tablespoons olive oil
6 medium tomatoes, thinly sliced
3/4 lb. fresh mushrooms, sliced
4 cups shredded mozzarella cheese (1 lb.)

Parmesan Pizza Crust:

Grated Parmesan cheese for pizza pans
2-2/3 cups all-purpose flour
1/3 cup freshly grated Parmesan cheese (1 oz.)
2-1/2 teaspoons baking powder

1 teaspoon salt
1/4 cup butter or margarine
1/4 cup lard
3/4 cup milk

Prepare and prebake Parmesan Pizza Crust. Leave oven set at 425°F (220°C). In a small bowl, combine garlic, Parmesan cheese, pine nuts, basil, parsley, salt and pepper; set aside. Gently spread each prebaked crust with 1 tablespoon of the olive oil. Make 1 layer on each crust with half of the tomato slices. Sprinkle with half of the Parmesan cheese mixture, half of the mushroom slices and half of the mozzarella cheese. Repeat layers. Bake 20 to 25 minutes in preheated oven until crust is browned and filling bubbles. Makes two 12-inch pizzas.

Parmesan Pizza Crust:

Preheat oven to 425°F (220°C). Butter two 12-inch pizza pans and dust with grated Parmesan cheese. In a large bowl, combine flour, 1/3 cup Parmesan cheese, baking powder and salt. Use a pastry blender or two knives to cut butter or margarine and lard into flour mixture. Gradually stir in milk; beat by hand or with electric mixer on low until mixture leaves the side of the bowl. Gather into a ball; knead 10 times while still in bowl. Divide dough in half and roll each half into a 13-inch circle on a lightly floured surface. Transfer to prepared pizza pans, crimping to make a slightly raised edge. Bake 9 minutes in preheated oven; cool 10 minutes on a rack. Makes two 12-inch pizza crusts.

Parmesan Pizza Crust Variation

Substitute 1/4 cup plus 1 tablespoon shortening for lard or 1/2 cup plus 2 tablespoons shortening for butter or margarine and lard.

White pepper is light in color and has a milder flavor than black pepper. Use it in dishes with a pale color or a delicate flavor.

Can't-Believe-It Quiche

As if by magic, this busy-day quiche separates into crust and filling as it bakes.

1/2 lb. bacon
1 cup shredded Swiss cheese (4 oz.)
1/2 cup finely chopped onion
2 cups milk
3 or 4 drops hot pepper sauce

1/2 cup biscuit mix
4 eggs
1/4 teaspoon salt
Paprika

Cook bacon until crisp in a medium skillet. Drain on paper towels; crumble. Preheat oven to 350°F (175°C). Lightly butter a 9-inch glass pie plate. Distribute crumbled bacon, cheese and onion evenly over bottom of prepared pie plate. In blender, beat milk, hot pepper sauce, biscuit mix, eggs and salt on high speed 1 minute or until blended and frothy. Pour over mixture in pie plate. Sprinkle with paprika. Bake 50 to 55 minutes in preheated oven until golden and a knife inserted off-center comes out clean. Let stand 5 minutes before cutting in wedges. Makes 6 servings.

Farmhouse Pizza

These two deep-dish double-crust pizzas have four cheeses in the filling. No tomatoes!

Egg-Rich Pizza Crust, see below
1 (10-oz.) pkg. frozen chopped spinach,
   cooked, drained
2 cups ricotta cheese (1 lb.)
1 cup shredded mozzarella cheese (4 oz.)
1/4 cup shredded provolone cheese (1 oz.)

1/4 cup freshly grated Romano cheese (3/4 oz.)
1/4 lb. Italian salami, chopped
2 eggs, slightly beaten
1/2 teaspoon salt
1/4 teaspoon ground nutmeg
1/8 teaspoon pepper

Egg-Rich Pizza Crust:
2 cups all-purpose flour
3/4 teaspoon salt
1/2 cup butter or margarine,
   room temperature

1/2 cup vegetable shortening
3 eggs, slightly beaten
1 tablespoon cold water

Prepare Egg-Rich Pizza Crust. Preheat oven to 375°F (190°C). In a large bowl, combine spinach, ricotta, mozzarella, provolone and Romano cheeses, salami, eggs, salt, nutmeg and pepper. Spoon half of the cheese mixture into each prepared crust. Place top crusts on each pizza. Trim edges 1/2-inch larger than pans, turn under and flute. Brush top crusts with egg mixture reserved from crust. Bake 1 hour in preheated oven until filling bubbles and crust browns. Makes two 9-inch pizzas.

Egg-Rich Pizza Crust:
Sift flour and salt into a large bowl. With a pastry blender or 2 knives, cut butter or margarine and shortening into flour and salt until crumbly. Measure 2 tablespoons of the beaten eggs into a small bowl. Add water; set aside. Add remaining beaten eggs to flour mixture. Mix lightly with a fork until pastry holds together and leaves side of bowl. Divide dough into 4 equal parts; shape into balls. On a lightly floured surface, roll out 2 balls of dough into 11-inch circles. Fit circles into two 9-inch pie pans. Roll remaining 2 balls of dough into two 12-inch circles. Cut small slits in center of each.

Springtime Quiche

Prebaking a lined pie shell filled with beans or rice is called baking blind. *See box on page 85.*

Pâte Brisée dough, from Holiday
Main-Dish Cheesecake, page 86
3 tablespoons butter or margarine
1 tablespoon vegetable oil
16 green onions with tops, thinly sliced
1 tablespoon flour

4 eggs, slightly beaten
1-1/3 cups half-and-half or light cream
1-3/4 cups shredded Gruyère cheese (7 oz.)
3/4 teaspoon salt
1 teaspoon dried oregano leaves, crumbled

Prepare Pâte Brisée dough. Do not roll out. Refrigerate at least 2 hours or overnight. Generously butter an 11-inch quiche pan; set aside. On a lightly floured surface, roll out Pâte Brisée dough. Fit loosely into prepared pan. Do not stretch dough. Trim pastry edge 1 inch larger than pan. Fold 3/4 inch under. Firmly press pastry against sides of pan. Pastry will extend 1/4 inch above edge of pan. Prick bottom and sides with a fork. Refrigerate pastry shell 30 minutes. Preheat oven to 400°F (205°C). Bake blind 12 minutes; see Baking Blind, page 85. Remove liner and beans or rice; prick pastry shell again. Bake 8 minutes longer. Cool on a rack while preparing filling. In a small saucepan, combine butter or margarine and oil. Stir in green onions and flour. Cook 5 minutes over medium heat, stirring constantly. In a medium bowl, combine eggs and cream. Stir in green onion mixture, cheese and salt. Pour into Pâte Brisée shell; sprinkle with oregano. Bake 30 to 40 minutes in preheated oven before serving. Makes 6 to 8 servings.

How to Make Farmhouse Pizza

1/Spoon spinach-cheese filling into 2 prepared crusts.

2/Add top crusts. Trim 1/2 inch larger than pans.

Big Thick-Crust Pizza

The perfect pizza for those who think a tasty, thick crust is more important than the filling.

Thick Pizza Crust, see below
Pizza Sauce, see below
1/2 lb. sweet or Hot Italian sausage, sliced,
   cooked, drained
1 green pepper, seeded, cut in thin strips

1 large onion, thinly sliced
1/2 lb. fresh mushrooms, thinly sliced
2 cups shredded Monterey Jack cheese (8 oz.)
1/3 cup freshly grated Parmesan cheese (1 oz.)

Thick Pizza Crust:
2 cups whole-wheat flour
1/4 cup wheat germ
1 pkg. active dry yeast (1 tablespoon)
3/4 teaspoon salt

1 tablespoon vegetable oil
1 tablespoon honey
1 cup very warm water (125°F, 50°C)

Pizza Sauce:
3 tablespoons olive oil
1/4 cup chopped onion
2 garlic cloves, minced
1 (28-oz.) can Italian plum tomatoes in
   tomato sauce

1 (6-oz.) can tomato paste
1 tablespoon dried basil leaves, crumbled
1 teaspoon dried oregano leaves, crumbled
1 teaspoon salt
1/2 teaspoon sugar

Prepare Thick Pizza Crust and Pizza Sauce. Preheat oven to 425°F (220°C). Spread 1 cup Pizza Sauce evenly over crust, leaving edges clear. Reserve remaining sauce for another use. Top with sausage, green pepper strips, onion and mushrooms. Sprinkle evenly with Monterey Jack cheese and Parmesan cheese. Bake 20 minutes on bottom rack of preheated oven until crust is golden and cheeses bubble. Makes 1 pizza.

Thick Pizza Crust:
Lightly oil a 15-1/2" x 10-1/2" jelly-roll pan; set aside. Combine flour, wheat germ, dry yeast and salt in a medium bowl. Stir in oil, honey and water. Do not add more flour; do not knead. Dough will be soft and sticky. Let dough rest 10 minutes. Turn into prepared pan. Lightly oil hands. With hands, pat and spread gently until dough covers pan, leaving edges slightly thicker than center.

Pizza Sauce:
Heat olive oil in a 3-quart saucepan. Add onion and garlic. Cook and stir over moderate heat until soft but not browned. Add remaining ingredients, breaking up tomatoes with a spoon. Reduce heat and simmer uncovered until thick, 45 to 50 minutes, stirring often. Makes about 3-1/2 cups.

You'll get optimum flavor from dried herb leaves by crumbling them in the palm of your hand.

Daria's Artichoke Quiche

Wheat germ adds a nutty taste to the crust.

Wheat Germ Pastry, see below
1 (10-oz.) can artichoke hearts,
   packed in water
2 tablespoons vegetable oil
1/4 cup minced onion
1/4 cup snipped fresh parsley
1-1/4 cups shredded Danish Esrom cheese
   (5 oz.)
3/4 cup freshly grated Parmesan cheese
   (2-1/4 oz.)

2 cups ricotta cheese (8 oz.)
2/3 cup dairy sour cream
5 eggs, slightly beaten
2 teaspoons dried dill weed
1/2 teaspoon ground nutmeg
1 teaspoon salt
1/2 teaspoon white pepper

Wheat Germ Pastry:
1 (11-oz.) pkg. pie crust mix
1/4 cup wheat germ

5 to 6 tablespoons cold water
1 egg, beaten

Prepare and refrigerate Wheat Germ Pastry at least 1 hour before continuing with quiche. Preheat oven to 400°F (205°C). Remove pastry shell from refrigerator; spread artichoke hearts evenly over bottom of shell. Heat oil in a small skillet over medium-low heat. Sauté onion and parsley 5 minutes; sprinkle over artichoke hearts. Combine Esrom and Parmesan cheeses; spread evenly over artichoke hearts and onion mixture. Combine ricotta cheese and sour cream in a large bowl. Beat to blend. Stir in eggs, dill weed, nutmeg, salt and white pepper. Pour into pastry shell. Bake quiche and pastry circles 10 minutes in preheated oven; remove pastry circles. Reduce oven temperature to 350°F (175°C). Bake quiche about 40 minutes longer until knife inserted off-center comes out clean. Place cooked pastry circles on top of filling; bake 5 minutes longer. Cool 5 minutes before cutting into wedges. Makes 6 to 8 servings.

Wheat Germ Pastry:
In a medium bowl, combine pie crust mix and wheat germ. Beat 5 tablespoons water and egg together in a small bowl. Pour over wheat germ mixture. Lightly toss with a fork until mixture holds together and leaves side of bowl. Add 1 tablespoon water if needed. On a lightly floured surface, roll out 2/3 dough 1/8-inch thick. Fit into an 11-inch quiche pan; refrigerate. Roll out remaining dough. Cut into circles or other small decorative shapes. Place on an ungreased baking sheet; set aside to bake with quiche. Makes 1 single pastry shell and 7 to 10 decorative shapes.

———————————————— •••• ————————————————

Brushing egg on unbaked pie shells keeps the lower crust from getting soggy during baking. See Greek Spinach Pie, page 78.

Little Onion Tarts

Individual pies have cheese in the custard and in the airy topping.

Standard Pastry for Cheese Pies,
  Double-Crust, page 77
2 tablespoons butter or margarine
1/2 cup chopped onion
4 eggs, separated
1-1/2 cups dairy sour cream

1/4 teaspoon salt
1/8 teaspoon pepper
2 tablespoons grated Parmesan cheese
1/2 lb. Gruyère cheese, cut in 1/2-inch cubes
1 tablespoon finely snipped celery leaves

Preheat oven to 450°F (230°C). Mix pastry according to directions; roll out half of dough 1/8-inch thick. Using a saucer as a pattern, cut three 6-inch rounds. Repeat with remaining dough. Fit each round into a 4-inch tart pan; do not stretch dough. Trim edges 1/2-inch larger than pans. Turn edges under and flute to make standing borders. Prick shell bottoms and sides with a sharp-tined fork. Bake 5 minutes; remove from oven and set aside. Reduce oven temperature to 325°F (165°C). Melt butter or margarine in a small skillet. Add onion and sauté until soft but not browned. Spoon sautéed onion into prepared shells, dividing evenly. In a medium bowl, slightly beat egg yolks. Stir in sour cream, salt, pepper and Parmesan cheese. Set aside 18 Gruyère cheese cubes. Fold remaining cubes into egg mixture. Spoon over onion in tart shells. Bake 15 minutes in preheated oven. While tarts bake, beat egg whites to soft peaks. Remove tarts from oven. Spoon egg whites over tops, spreading with the back of the spoon. Place 3 of the reserved cheese cubes on top of each tart. Bake 10 minutes longer until tarts are golden brown and cheese cubes have melted. Let stand 5 minutes. Sprinkle with snipped celery leaves before serving. Makes six 4-inch tarts.

How to Make Little Onion Tarts

1/Press pastry into tart pans, trim edges, turn under and flute to make standing borders.

2/Use back of a spoon to spread egg whites over cheese filling. Top each with 3 cheese cubes.

Cheese & Vegetable Pie Italian-Style

Pleasantly flavored green-ripe olives can be found with ripe olives in the supermarket.

2 tablespoons olive oil
2 medium zucchini, thinly sliced
2 medium onions, thinly sliced
1/2 teaspoon salt
1 tablespoon olive oil
1 garlic clove, crushed
3 tablespoons snipped fresh parsley
1 (1-lb.) can whole tomatoes, coarsely chopped
1 (8-oz.) can tomato sauce
1 teaspoon sugar
1/2 teaspoon dried oregano leaves, crumbled
1/8 teaspoon pepper

1/2 teaspoon salt
2 cups ricotta cheese (1 lb.)
4 eggs
1/2 teaspoon salt
1-1/2 cups milk
1 (8-oz.) tube refrigerated crescent rolls,
   unrolled, separated
1/4 lb. sliced mozzarella cheese
1 (2-oz.) can rolled anchovy fillets with capers,
   drained
3/4 cup pitted green-ripe olives, halved

Heat 2 tablespoons olive oil in a large skillet. Add zucchini, onions and 1/2 teaspoon salt. Cook and stir over medium heat until tender, about 10 minutes. Remove zucchini mixture from skillet with a slotted spoon and set aside. Pour 1 tablespoon olive oil into skillet. Add garlic and parsley. Sauté 1 minute, stirring constantly. Add tomatoes, tomato sauce, sugar, oregano, pepper and 1/2 teaspoon salt. Cook 15 minutes, stirring often. Set aside and keep warm. Preheat oven to 375°F (190°C). In a large bowl, beat together ricotta cheese, eggs and 1/2 teaspoon salt. Gradually beat in milk; set aside. Line a 10-inch quiche pan or pie pan with crescent roll triangles, overlapping slightly. Press edges of triangles together; do not prick. Spread zucchini mixture on bottom of lined pan. Spoon about 1/4 cup of the warm tomato mixture over zucchini mixture. Pour in ricotta cheese mixture. Bake 40 minutes in preheated oven until softly set in center. Arrange mozzarella cheese slices on top of pie. Reserve 1 cup of the tomato mixture. Spoon remaining tomato mixture around cheese slices. Bake about 8 minutes longer until cheese is melted. Top with anchovies and olives. Cut in wedges to serve. Reheat reserved tomato mixture. Spoon over each serving. Makes 6 to 8 servings.

Baking Blind

Gently fit prepared pastry into a pie pan, fluting the edge as desired. Lightly prick the pastry shell bottom and side. Being careful not to tear the pastry, press a single piece of lightweight foil, waxed paper or parchment paper into the pastry shell. Pour dry beans or rice into the liner 1/2 inch deep. Or pour beans or rice into an oven-roasting bag and fit into the pastry shell. Bake as recipe directs. Store beans or rice in roasting bag or other container and use for future baking blind.

Holiday Main-Dish Cheesecake

Delicious, unusual and—best of all—economical. This will serve a hungry crowd.

Pâte Brisée, see below
4 cups cream-style cottage cheese (2 lbs.)
1/4 cup all-purpose flour
1/4 cup minced onion
1/2 teaspoon salt
1/2 teaspoon dried oregano leaves, crumbled

3 to 4 drops hot pepper sauce
5 eggs
1/2 cup freshly grated Parmesan cheese
   (1-1/2 oz.)
1/2 cup snipped fresh parsley
1/2 cup chopped pepperoni sausage (3 oz.)

Pâte Brisée:
1 cup all-purpose flour
1/4 cup butter or margarine,
   room temperature

1 egg yolk
Cold water, if required

Prepare Pâte Brisée. Set aside to cool. Reduce oven heat to 400°F (205°C). In a large bowl, beat cottage cheese until smooth. Stir in flour, onion, salt, oregano and hot pepper sauce. Add eggs one at a time, beating well after each addition. Stir in Parmesan cheese, parsley and sausage. Turn into prebaked Pâte Brisée shell. Bake 10 minutes in preheated oven. Reduce heat to 325°F (165°C). Bake 60 to 70 minutes longer until a knife inserted off-center comes out clean. Cool 10 minutes; remove rim of springform pan. Cut in wedges to serve. Makes 10 to 12 servings.

Pâte Brisée:
In a small bowl, blend flour, butter or margarine and egg yolk with a fork. If necessary, add 1 to 2 tablespoons cold water to hold dough together. Cover and refrigerate 1 hour. Preheat oven to 425°F (220°C). Butter the rim, but not the bottom, of a 9-inch springform pan. Divide refrigerated dough in half. On a lightly floured surface, roll out half of the dough to a 9-inch circle 1/8-inch thick to cover the bottom of the pan. Transfer to pan bottom; trim. Insert pan bottom into prepared rim. Roll out remaining half of the dough to a 12" x 1-1/2" rectangle. Cut lengthwise into two 12" x 3/4" strips. Press strips around inside bottom of pan rim, overlapping to join. Press strips of dough and bottom together. Bake 10 to 12 minutes in preheated oven until golden brown. Remove from oven and cool slightly. Press crust edge gently against rim of pan if it has shrunk during baking.

There is no need to sift pre-sifted flour, but it should be stirred before measuring.

Side Dishes

Cheese transforms rice, pasta, fritters, eggs, dumplings and spoon bread into dinner-table triumphs and gives vegetables a new lease on life. Mix cheese, eggs and flour with potatoes to make Genoa-Style Gnocchi. Add cheese and a little fruit to cornmeal for Teleme Polenta. Stuff artichokes with a cheese-rich dressing and you have Roman Artichokes.

Vegetables are easy to prepare in new and different ways. *Panning* or *braising* is similar to sautéing. To *pan* vegetables, remove cores and firm ribs, peel if necessary, then slice or chop the vegetables. Toss them in melted butter or margarine in a large wok or large heavy skillet over medium heat until they just begin to wilt. Add a small amount of water to prevent burning. Sprinkle shredded cheese over the hot vegetables as they are served.

Hot Swiss Cucumbers are a new and different stuffed vegetable. Remove seeds from peeled cucumber halves with the tip of a teaspoon. Soften the cucumbers by *parboiling* them in hot broth before they are stuffed and baked. Parboiling means to cook in liquid until just tender.

Omelets are served with every meal and make perfect side dishes when vegetables or meat are added. Baked Omelet Santa Fe is a special Southwestern side dish. The secret to this high, light and puffy omelet is stiffly-beaten egg whites. When egg whites are beaten, air is captured in pockets of foam. Continue beating them until soft peaks form with the tips of the peaks bending over slightly. Add cream of tartar at this point to firm the walls of the air pockets. Then beat the whites until stiff. As the omelet cooks, air expands, stretching the air pockets and adding volume. If egg whites are beaten stiff without a stabilizer such as cream of tartar, they separate and shrink. Adding salt to egg whites causes them to separate rather than hold their shape.

Sunday Brunch

Cinnamon-Spiced Grapefruit Juice
Turkey Cutlets, Norwegian-Style, page 71
Hot Swiss Cucumbers, page 91
Tossed Green Salad
Blue Cheese Vinaigrette, page 45
Chocolate Bliss, page 134
French Gruyère Braids, page 112

Cheddary Onions

Use leftover chopped onion centers in other baked dishes.

4 large mild white onions
Water
1-1/2 cups shredded sharp Cheddar cheese
   (6 oz.)
1/4 lb. fresh mushrooms, chopped
1 cup soft white breadcrumbs, page 108
1/4 teaspoon dried oregano leaves, crumbled
1/4 teaspoon dried thyme leaves, crumbled
Salt and pepper to taste
2 tablespoons butter or margarine

1 tablespoon all-purpose flour
2 tablespoons snipped fresh parsley
1 cup milk
2 tablespoons dry sherry or milk
1/4 teaspoon salt
Pepper to taste
1/4 cup freshly grated Parmesan cheese,
   (3/4 oz.)
2 tablespoons snipped fresh parsley
1/2 teaspoon paprika

Lightly butter a 9" x 9" baking dish; set aside. Place unpeeled onions and water to cover in a 5-quart pot or Dutch oven. Bring to a boil and cook 20 minutes. Drain and set aside to cool. Peel cooled onions, cutting off roots and stems. Push out center of each onion leaving a 1/2-inch shell; reserve centers. Preheat oven to 375°F (190°C). Place onions in prepared baking dish. Finely chop reserved onion centers. Combine 1 cup chopped onions, Cheddar cheese, mushrooms, breadcrumbs, oregano, thyme and salt and pepper to taste. Spoon onion stuffing into onion shells. Cover and bake 1 hour in preheated oven until onions are tender when pierced with a fork. Melt butter or margarine in a small saucepan over medium-low heat. Stir in flour until mixture is smooth and bubbly. Add 2 tablespoons parsley, 1 cup milk and 2 tablespoons sherry or milk. Cook and stir until sauce bubbles and thickens. Season with 1/4 teaspoon salt and pepper to taste. Combine Parmesan cheese, 2 table-spoons parsley and paprika in a small bowl. Remove onions from oven and cover with sauce. Sprinkle with Parmesan cheese mixture. Serve immediately. Makes 4 servings.

Panned Lettuce Dutch-Style

Panning is like sautéing with a little water added and the pan covered.

2 heads iceberg lettuce (about 1 lb.)
2 tablespoons butter or margarine

Salt and coarsely ground black pepper to taste
1-1/4 cups shredded Edam cheese (5 oz.)

Cut cores from heads of lettuce. Cut each head of lettuce into 6 wedges; cut each wedge in half crosswise. Melt butter or margarine over medium heat in a large wok or large heavy skillet. Add lettuce. Cover and steam 1 minute until lettuce wedges on bottom of pan turn bright green and begin to wilt. Stir lettuce. Cover and steam 1 minute longer. Spoon panned lettuce into a warm serving dish. Season with salt and pepper to taste. Sprinkle with cheese; toss lightly to distribute cheese. Serve immediately. Makes 4 to 6 servings.

Variation

Substitute 1 pound spinach or young cabbage for lettuce.

Mediterranean Medley

Asiago cheese has a stronger flavor than Swiss, Gruyère or Appenzeller.

2 medium eggplants
3 tablespoons salt
2 cups grated Asiago cheese (6 oz.)
1 cup fine dry breadcrumbs, page 108
1 tablespoon snipped fresh oregano or
   1 teaspoon dried oregano leaves, crumbled
3 to 5 tablespoons vegetable oil

2 large zucchini, sliced
1/2 lb. fresh mushrooms, sliced
5 large tomatoes, sliced
10 oz. fresh spinach, washed, stems removed
   (1 bunch)
1 large green pepper, seeded, cut in strips
Salt and freshly ground black pepper to taste

Peel eggplants; cut into 1/2-inch slices. Generously sprinkle both sides of eggplant slices with 3 tablespoons salt. Drain in a colander 30 minutes. Rinse well and pat dry with paper towels. Combine cheese, breadcrumbs and oregano in a medium bowl; set aside. Preheat oven to 375°F (190°C). Lightly butter a 5-quart casserole dish. Heat 3 tablespoons oil in a large skillet. Sauté rinsed eggplant slices in oil until lightly browned, adding more oil if necessary. Layer half of each vegetable in casserole, sprinkling each layer with about 3 tablespoons cheese mixture and salt and pepper to taste. Repeat layering with remaining vegetables. Top with remaining cheese mixture. Bake uncovered 30 to 40 minutes in preheated oven until vegetables are tender. Makes 12 to 14 servings.

Baked Omelet Santa Fe

Puffy and light, this two-cheese dish is marvelous with a barbecued leg of lamb.

3-1/2 cups shredded Monterey Jack cheese
   (14 oz.)
3-1/2 cups shredded sharp Cheddar cheese
   (14 oz.)
1 cup thinly sliced green onions with
   some tops
2 medium tomatoes, seeded, chopped
1/4 cup chopped green chile peppers, drained
1 (2-1/4-oz.) can sliced ripe olives, drained

1/2 cup all-purpose flour
6 eggs, separated
1 (5-1/4-oz.) can evaporated milk,
   undiluted (3/4 cup)
1/2 teaspoon salt
1/2 teaspoon dried oregano leaves, crumbled
1/4 teaspoon ground cumin
1/4 teaspoon cream of tartar

Preheat oven to 300°F (150°C). Generously butter a shallow 3-quart casserole dish; set aside. In a large bowl, combine Monterey Jack cheese, Cheddar cheese, green onions, tomatoes, green chiles, olives and 2 tablespoons flour. Toss to distribute flour; spoon into prepared casserole dish. In a small bowl, beat egg yolks with a fork until frothy. Alternately add milk and remaining flour, beating until smooth. Stir in salt, oregano and cumin. In a large bowl, beat egg whites with cream of tartar until stiff moist peaks form. Fold egg yolk mixture into beaten egg whites. Spoon egg mixture over cheese mixture. Bake 60 minutes in preheated oven until top is golden brown and firm. Serve immediately. Makes 8 to 10 servings.

Hot Swiss Cucumbers

Here is a new and different vegetable dish that everyone will enjoy.

1 teaspoon instant chicken broth granules	1/2 teaspoon dried marjoram leaves, crumbled
1 cup water	1 egg, slightly beaten
3 large cucumbers, peeled	1/8 teaspoon pepper
2 tablespoons butter or margarine	1 cup shredded Swiss cheese (4 oz.)
1/2 cup chopped radishes	1 teaspoon dried parsley leaves
2 cups soft white breadcrumbs, page 108	

Combine instant chicken broth granules and water in a large skillet over medium-high heat. Cut cucumbers in half lengthwise. Using the tip of a teaspoon, scoop out and discard seeds. Place cucumber halves cut-side down in broth. Cover skillet and bring broth to a boil. Reduce heat and simmer 15 minutes. Preheat oven to 350°F (175°C). Generously butter a 10" x 6" baking dish. Remove cucumbers from broth with a slotted spoon. Place on paper towels to drain. Reserve broth. Melt butter or margarine in the same skillet. Add radishes and sauté until soft. Stir in breadcrumbs, marjoram, egg, pepper and reserved broth. Stir in 1/2 cup of the cheese until melted. Arrange cucumber halves cut-side up in prepared baking dish. Fill hollow centers of cucumbers with stuffing mixture. Bake 20 minutes in preheated oven. In a small bowl, combine remaining cheese with parsley; sprinkle over cucumbers. Bake 20 minutes longer. Makes 6 servings.

How to Make Hot Swiss Cucumbers

1/Cut cucumbers in half and use a teaspoon to scoop out seeds.

2/Spoon stuffing into hollowed out centers of par-boiled cucumber halves.

Parmesan Fritters

Serve with chicken or ham or leave out the mustard and cheese and you have cream puff pastry!

6 tablespoons butter or margarine
1/2 teaspoon salt
1 cup water
1-1/4 cups all-purpose flour
4 eggs

1 teaspoon prepared mustard
1-1/2 cups freshly grated Parmesan cheese
  (4-1/2 oz.)
Oil for deep-frying

Combine butter or margarine, salt and water in a heavy saucepan. Stir constantly over high heat until butter is melted and mixture comes to a boil. Reduce heat to moderate. Add flour all at once, stirring vigorously until mixture is smooth. Continue stirring vigorously 5 or 6 seconds until mixture forms a ball. Add eggs one at a time, beating well after each addition. Remove from heat; beat a few seconds longer. Stir in mustard and 1 cup of the cheese. Let stand until lukewarm. Preheat oven to 200°F (95°C). Pour oil 3 inches deep into a deep-fryer or heavy saucepan and heat to 375°F 190°C). At this temperature a 1-inch cube of bread will turn golden brown in 40 seconds. Carefully lower fritter mixture into hot oil by teaspoonfuls. Cook a few at a time 4 to 5 minutes, turning every minute or so until puffed and golden brown. With a slotted spoon, place fritters on paper towels to drain. Place on baking sheet or ovenproof platter in preheated oven to keep warm. To serve, arrange on a warm platter and sprinkle with remaining 1/2 cup cheese. Makes 6 servings.

Genoa-Style Gnocchi

Tender little potato-cheese dumplings are perfect with veal scallops or chops.

6 medium potatoes, peeled
Water
1/2 teaspoon salt
2 eggs, well-beaten
1 teaspoon salt
3 cups all-purpose flour

1 (10-3/4-oz.) can condensed chicken broth
8 cups hot water
1/2 teaspoon dried thyme leaves, crumbled
1/2 cup butter or margarine, melted
1 cup freshly grated Parmesan cheese (3 oz.)

Lightly butter an 11" x 7" baking dish. In a large saucepan over medium-high heat, cook potatoes in 2 inches water and 1/2 teaspoon salt until tender when pierced with a fork. Drain; toss potatoes in saucepan over very low heat 2 minutes to dry. Mash potatoes in a large bowl until smooth. Beat in eggs and 1 teaspoon salt. Blend in flour to make a soft dough. Cover and refrigerate at least 1 hour. Bring broth, 8 cups hot water and thyme to a boil in a large pot. Preheat oven to 400°F (205°C). Carefully lower potato mixture by teaspoonfuls into boiling liquid. Simmer a few at a time until slightly puffed, about 5 minutes. Remove puffed gnocchi from boiling liquid with a slotted spoon. Place in prepared baking dish. Repeat until all potato mixture is used. Drizzle gnocchi with melted butter or margarine; sprinkle with Parmesan cheese. Bake 15 minutes in preheated oven until puffed and golden. Serve immediately. Makes 8 servings.

Roman Artichokes

To snip parsley, cut it into tiny pieces with scissors or kitchen shears.

2 cups coarse white breadcrumbs, page 108
1/2 cup snipped fresh parsley
3/4 cup freshly grated Romano cheese
  (2-1/4 oz.)
1 tablespoon minced onion
1 garlic clove, minced
3/4 teaspoon salt

1/8 teaspoon pepper
4 large artichokes
4 tablespoons olive oil
Boiling water
1 cup butter or margarine, melted
1 large lemon cut in 4 wedges

Place breadcrumbs, parsley, cheese, onion, garlic, salt and pepper in a medium bowl. Toss lightly to combine; set aside. Rinse artichokes; cut off stems even with base. Cut off about 1 inch of artichoke tops with a sharp knife. With kitchen scissors, snip off all spiny leaf tips. Gently spread leaves open; pull out small yellow inner leaves. With a teaspoon, scrape out fuzzy choke just below inner leaves. Spoon stuffing mixture into hollow centers of artichokes. Place stuffed artichokes in a deep kettle stem-side down. Spoon 1 tablespoon olive oil over each artichoke. Carefully pour boiling water 2 inches deep into kettle. Cover and bring water to a boil again. Reduce heat; simmer until artichoke leaves easily pull away from base, about 40 minutes. Drain on paper towels stem-side down. Pour 1/4 cup melted butter or margarine into each of 4 small bowls. Let diners squeeze lemon juice over cooked artichoke and stuffing if desired. Eat stuffing with a fork. Pull leaves from artichokes with fingers; dip lower part of leaves into melted butter, then pull meaty portion off leaves with lower teeth. Makes 4 servings.

Alpine Dairy Scallop

Thin slices of potato are layered with cream and cheese that melts into a glorious sauce.

6 medium potatoes, peeled, cut in thin slices
1-1/2 cups shredded Appenzeller cheese (6 oz.)
Salt and pepper to taste
1 cup heavy cream or whipping cream
2 tablespoons grated onion

1/4 cup freshly grated Parmesan cheese
  (3/4 oz.)
1 tablespoon paprika
1 tablespoon snipped fresh parsley

Preheat oven to 325°F (165°C). Lightly butter a 13" x 9" baking dish. Layer 1/3 of the potato slices in prepared baking dish. Top with 1/3 of the Appenzeller cheese; sprinkle with salt and pepper to taste. Make 2 more layers of potato slices and Appenzeller cheese. Stir cream and onion together. Pour evenly over layered potatoes and cheese. Combine Parmesan cheese and paprika in a small bowl; sprinkle over casserole. Bake 2 hours in preheated oven until potatoes are tender and liquid is absorbed. Garnish with snipped parsley. Makes 6 servings.

Variation

Substitute Gruyère or Swiss cheese for Appenzeller cheese. Undiluted evaporated milk may be substituted for cream.

Chile-Jack Casserole

If you prefer converted or parboiled rice, prepare it according to package directions.

2-1/2 cups water
1/2 teaspoon salt
1-1/4 cups long-grain white rice, uncooked
2 tablespoons butter or margarine
1/2 cup finely chopped onion
1/2 teaspoon salt

1 cup half-and-half or light cream
1/2 lb. Monterey Jack cheese, cubed
1 (4-oz.) can chopped green chile peppers
2 cups dairy sour cream
Paprika

Bring water and 1/2 teaspoon salt to a boil in a medium saucepan over medium-high heat. Slowly add rice, being sure water continues to boil. Cover and turn heat to low. Cook 30 to 40 minutes until most of the liquid is absorbed and rice is tender and fluffy; set aside. Preheat oven to 325°F (165°C). Lightly butter a 2-quart casserole; set aside. Melt butter or margarine in a small skillet. Add onion; sauté until soft but not browned. Remove from heat; stir in 1/2 teaspoon salt and half-and-half or light cream. In prepared casserole dish, layer 1/3 each of the cooked rice, onion mixture, cheese, chile peppers, and sour cream. Repeat to make 2 more layers. Sprinkle with paprika. Bake about 30 minutes in preheated oven until bubbling hot. Makes 6 servings.

Teleme Polenta

Polenta *with pine nuts or* pignolias *is a popular Italian cornmeal mush served with vegetables.*

1/4 cup butter or margarine
1-3/4 cups finely chopped onions
2 cups water
1/2 teaspoon salt
1 cup yellow cornmeal
2 cups cold water

1 lb. teleme cheese, cut in 1/4-inch slices
1/2 cup toasted pine nuts
1/4 cup golden raisins
1/4 cup butter or margarine
3 tablespoons grated Parmesan cheese
3 tablespoons snipped fresh parsley

Butter a shallow 2-quart baking dish; set aside. Melt 1/4 cup butter or margarine in a medium skillet. Add onions; sauté until soft but not browned. Bring 2 cups water and 1/2 teaspoon salt to a boil in a large saucepan. Combine cornmeal and 2 cups cold water in a medium bowl. Stir cornmeal mixture into boiling water using a whisk. Stir constantly over medium heat until mixture returns to a boil; cook 5 minutes longer. Remove from heat; stir in sautéed onions. Preheat oven to 350°F (175°C). Spread half of the cornmeal mixture in prepared baking dish. Top with half of the teleme cheese slices, half of the pine nuts and all of the raisins. Cover with remaining cornmeal mixture, teleme cheese slices and nuts. Melt 1/4 cup butter or margarine in skillet; pour over top of unbaked polenta. Sprinkle with Parmesan cheese. Bake 50 minutes in preheated oven. Let stand 5 minutes; cut into squares. Garnish with snipped parsley. Makes 6 servings.

Variation

Substitute Monterey Jack cheese for teleme cheese. Substitute chopped peanuts for pine nuts.

Welsh Gratin

Leeks look like onions with thick tough stalks. Always cook them before serving.

2 lbs. leeks or 6 to 8 bunches green onions
Water
1/2 teaspoon salt
2 tablespoons butter or margarine
2 tablespoons all-purpose flour

1/2 cup half-and-half or light cream
1/2 cup chicken broth
1 cup shredded Gruyère cheese (4 oz.)
1/4 teaspoon ground nutmeg
3 tablespoons crushed seasoned croutons

Cut off root ends and brown or damaged greens from leeks or onions. Wash under cold running water with root-end down. Tie into 2 bundles with kitchen string. Bring water and salt to a boil in a large kettle. Add leek or onion bundles. Cook 10 to 15 minutes until tender. Drain; remove string. Preheat oven to 375°F (190°C). Lightly butter a shallow casserole dish or gratin dish. Arrange cooked leeks or onions in prepared dish; set aside. Melt butter or margarine in a small saucepan over medium-low heat. Stir in flour until mixture is smooth and bubbly. Stir in cream and broth until mixture bubbles and thickens. Blend in nutmeg and 3/4 cup of the cheese. Stir until cheese melts. Pour cheese sauce over leeks or onions. Sprinkle with remaining cheese and crushed croutons. Bake 15 to 20 minutes in preheated oven until lightly browned. Makes 6 servings.

How to Make Teleme Polenta

1/Use a whisk to stir cornmeal and water mixture into boiling salted water. Cook until thickened.

2/Spread remaining cornmeal mixture over half of cheese slices, half of nuts and all of raisins.

Cheese Specialties

Cheese specialties depend on cheese for their very being. One such dish is elegant and satisfying rabbit—sometimes called *rarebit*. A good rabbit is smooth and medium thick. Pungent cheese is melted into a milk, cream, beer or wine sauce. Although most rabbits are made with *Cheddar* cheese, Port & Walnut Rabbit contains England's wonderful *Wensleydale*, a delicious blue-veined cheese that melts like a Cheddar cheese. Rabbits are served over toast, crackers, biscuits, bread or in toast cups. In this recipe, rabbit is served over Walnut Toast—triangles of walnut sandwiches sautéed until golden brown.

There are several unusual fondues in this section. One is made with beer, another with anchovies, and a very special one—Dieter's Delight—is prepared with low-fat cheese and low-fat or skim milk. It is festive and delicious while meeting the requirements of low-fat, low-calorie and diabetic diets. Low-fat cheese is available in brick form or as a spread. Either may be used in this recipe. If you use the spread, reduce the amount of milk by about 3 tablespoons. Broccoli flowerets, raw mushroom caps, zucchini and carrot slices are fine low-calorie dippers.

Unusual and delicious desserts round out this section. Paskha is a Russian Easter dessert, elegant, nutritious and easily prepared. Paskha molds made of wood and in the traditional truncated or flattened pyramid shape are available in specialty shops but are not necessary. You can pack the drained cottage cheese mixture into a plastic or unglazed-clay flower pot as long as it has a hole in the bottom.

Backyard Cookout
Grilled Rib-Eye Steaks
Crostini alla Roma, page 98
Cheddary Onions, page 88
Spinach-Mushroom Salad
Coconut Cake or Melon Wedges
Great Blueberry Swirl, page 108

Ringtum Diddy

Day-old bread will hold its shape in the custard cups better than fresh bread.

8 Toast Cups, see below
1 cup chopped onions
1/4 cup butter or margarine, melted
1 (10-3/4-oz.) can condensed tomato soup
1/2 cup milk

4 cups shredded sharp Cheddar cheese (1 lb.)
1 egg, slightly beaten
1/2 teaspoon Worcestershire sauce
2 drops hot pepper sauce

Toast Cups:
1/4 cup butter or margarine
1/4 cup half-and-half or light cream

8 slices white bread, crusts removed

Prepare Toast Cups; set aside. In a 10-inch skillet over medium heat, sauté onions in butter or margarine until soft but not browned. Stir in soup and milk until heated through. Add cheese 1 cup at a time, stirring after each addition until cheese is melted. Blend 1/2 cup cheese mixture into egg. Vigorously stir egg mixture into remaining cheese mixture. Do not boil. Place toast cups on individual serving dishes. Spoon cheese mixture into and around toast cups. Makes 8 servings.

Toast Cups:
Preheat oven to 375°F (190°C). Lightly butter eight 10-ounce custard cups or large muffin cups. Melt butter or margarine in a 10-inch skillet. Slowly stir in cream. Quickly dip bread in and out of cream mixture, coating both sides. Press into prepared cups. Bake about 10 minutes in preheated oven until lightly browned and crisp on edges. Remove baked toast cups from containers immediately.

Munich Fondue

Dark beer is not as bitter as light beer, but either can be used in this recipe.

1-1/2 cups buttermilk
1/2 cup dark beer
4 cups shredded Muenster cheese (1 lb.)
1 tablespoon cornstarch
2 teaspoons brown prepared mustard
Salt to taste

1/2 loaf rye bread
12 cocktail-sized smoked sausages,
   cooked, drained
8 cherry tomatoes
2 cups sliced raw cauliflowerets
1-1/2 cups green pepper strips

Stir buttermilk and beer in a medium saucepan over medium heat until bubbles appear around edge of pan. In a medium bowl, toss cheese and cornstarch until cheese is coated. Stir cheese mixture into buttermilk mixture 1 cup at a time until smooth. Continue to stir over medium heat until mixture begins to just bubble. Do not boil. Stir in prepared mustard and salt to taste. Pour mixture into a fondue pot or chafing dish; keep warm. Cut rye bread into 1-inch cubes. To serve, place sausages, tomatoes, cauliflowerets, green pepper strips and rye bread cubes in individual serving dishes. Using fondue forks, dip sausages, vegetables and bread cubes into fondue. Makes 4 to 6 servings.

Paskha

You'll need a tall narrow mold for this beautiful Russian Easter dessert.

3 (12-oz.) pkgs. large-curd cream-style
   cottage cheese (4-1/2 cups)
1/2 cup chopped mixed candied fruit
1 teaspoon vanilla extract
1 cup unsalted butter, room temperature
3/4 cup heavy cream or whipping cream
4 egg yolks

1 whole egg
3/4 cup sugar
1/2 cup finely chopped blanched almonds
5 candied red cherries, quartered
10 whole blanched almonds
3 dried apricots, cut in 18 strips

Place a colander in a large bowl. Turn cottage cheese into colander. Fit a plate into colander to press down cottage cheese. Weight plate with a 29-ounce can of food. Refrigerate 3 hours. Cut 2 layers of cheesecloth 14 inches square; set aside. In a small bowl, combine mixed candied fruit and vanilla; set aside. Discard cheese drippings. Turn pressed cottage cheese into a large bowl. Beat with electric mixer until smooth, increasing speed from medium to high. On medium speed, beat in butter until smooth; set aside. Pour cream into top of a double boiler. Place directly over medium heat until small bubbles appear around edge. Remove from heat. In a small bowl, beat egg yolks and whole egg until thickened. Gradually beat in sugar until mixture is pale yellow. Slowly beat in hot cream until blended. Pour cream mixture back into top of double boiler. Pour hot water 2 inches deep in bottom of double boiler. Bring to a simmer. Stir cream mixture over simmering water until it becomes a **very thick custard**, about 20 minutes. Remove from heat. Stir in candied fruit mixture. Place top of double boiler in a pan of ice cubes. Stir constantly until custard is cooled, about 5 minutes. With a rubber spatula, stir cooled custard and chopped almonds into cheese mixture. Wet prepared cheesecloth in cold water. Wring out excess water. Line a pyramid shaped paskha mold or a 5-1/2-inch diameter, 9-inch deep plastic or clay flowerpot with a hole in the bottom. Place mold on a rack over a shallow dish. Pour cheese mixture into cheesecloth-lined mold. Fold excess cheesecloth over top. Place paskha mold cover or a heavy object on top of cheesecloth. Refrigerate overnight. Remove cover or heavy object. Turn back cheesecloth from top of mold. Invert onto a serving dish or a platter; remove mold. Gently peel off cheesecloth. Decorate paskha with cherries, whole blanched almonds and apricot strips. Makes 16 to 20 servings.

Crostini alla Roma

These crusty open-face sandwiches are just the thing to serve with a fresh green salad.

12 slices French bread, 1/4-inch thick
1/3 lb. mozzarella cheese, cut in 12 slices
6 anchovy fillets

1/4 cup butter or margarine
1 small garlic clove, pressed

Preheat oven to 400°F (205°C). Lightly grease a shallow oval or rectangular 4-cup baking dish. Overlap bread and cheese slices alternately in prepared baking dish. Bake 7 to 10 minutes in preheated oven until cheese melts. While bread and cheese are baking, cover anchovies with cold water. Soak about 4 minutes. Drain and chop. Melt butter or margarine in a small saucepan over medium heat. Stir in chopped anchovies and pressed garlic. Pour anchovy mixture evenly over bread and cheese as they come from oven. Serve immediately. Makes 4 to 6 servings.

Port & Walnut Rabbit

Wensleydale *is a pale, flaky English cheese with a pungent flavor.*

Walnut Toast, see below
4 cups shredded Wensleydale cheese (1 lb.)
2 tablespoons all-purpose flour
2/3 cup port wine
1/2 cup heavy cream or whipping cream
2 tablespoons butter or margarine

2 teaspoons Worcestershire sauce
1 teaspoon dry mustard
3 drops hot pepper sauce
2 egg yolks
2 firm-ripe tomatoes, cut in 8 wedges

Walnut Toast:
8 slices white bread, crusts removed
10 tablespoons butter or margarine,
    room temperature

1/2 cup ground black or English walnuts

Prepare Walnut Toast, set aside. Pour water 2 inches deep in bottom of a double boiler. Bring to a simmer over medium heat. In top of double boiler, toss cheese and flour together. Add wine, cream, butter or margarine, Worcestershire sauce, dry mustard and hot pepper sauce. Stir over simmering water until thickened. Remove from heat. Stir in egg yolks until blended. Pour equally into 4 ungreased 10-ounce ramekins or other small dishes. Place 2 tomato wedges opposite each other on each serving. Stand 2 toast triangles between tomato wedges. Place remaining toast triangles on a small serving dish. Makes 4 servings.

Walnut Toast:
Place bread slices on waxed paper. Using 8 tablespoons butter or margarine, butter both sides of bread. Sprinkle 1 side with chopped walnuts. Gently press walnuts into bread. Place 2 slices of bread together with walnuts between. Cut diagonally. Melt remaining 2 tablespoons butter or margarine in a small skillet. Sauté walnut sandwiches on both sides until golden. Cut each sandwich diagonally again.

Variations

Mellow Cheddar cheese may be used in place of the Wensleydale.

Use Madeira wine instead of port wine.

For a less sweet version, substitute dry sherry for the port wine.

For a very sweet version, substitute apple juice for the port wine.

Unbleached flour may be used in place of all-purpose flour without changing the measurement.

Cheddar Soufflé Roulade

This airy Cheddar cheese soufflé is rolled around a savory filling.

1/3 cup butter or margarine
6 tablespoons all-purpose flour
1/8 teaspoon cayenne pepper
3/4 teaspoon salt
1-1/4 cups milk
3/4 cup freshly grated Parmesan cheese
  (2-1/4 oz.)

1/2 cup shredded sharp Cheddar cheese
  (2 oz.)
7 eggs, separated, room temperature
1/4 teaspoon cream of tartar
Spinach-Cheddar Filling, see below
1/4 lb. sharp Cheddar cheese, sliced

Spinach-Cheddar Filling:

1/4 cup finely chopped onion
2 tablespoons butter or margarine
2 (10-oz.) pkgs. frozen chopped spinach,
  thawed, squeezed dry

1/4 teaspoon salt
1/4 cup shredded sharp Cheddar cheese
  (1 oz.)
1/2 cup dairy sour cream

Generously grease the bottom of a 15" x 10-1/2" baking sheet with raised edges. Line bottom with waxed paper. Lightly grease top of paper. Set baking sheet aside. Preheat oven to 350°F (175°C). Melt butter or margarine in a medium saucepan over medium heat. Stir in flour, cayenne pepper and salt until mixture is smooth. Gradually stir in milk until mixture boils. Reduce heat. Continue to stir until mixture thickens and leaves bottom of pan. Stir in 1/2 cup of the Parmesan cheese and all of the Cheddar cheese. Place egg whites and egg yolks in separate large bowls. Beat egg yolks with a fork. Beat in cheese mixture. With electric mixer on high speed, beat egg whites and cream of tartar until stiff peaks form. By hand, fold about 1/3 of the beaten egg whites into the egg yolk mixture. Fold in remaining beaten egg whites until no white remains. Spread over bottom of prepared baking sheet. Bake about 15 minutes in preheated oven until puffed and firm when pressed with fingertips. While roulade bakes, prepare Spinach-Cheddar Filling; set aside. Cut a 16" x 12" piece of waxed paper. Sprinkle with remaining 1/4 cup Parmesan cheese. Remove roulade from oven. Preheat broiler. With a spatula, loosen edges of roulade. Invert onto waxed paper. Gently peel paper from bottom of roulade; discard paper. Spread surface of roulade with filling. Starting on a long side, lift from waxed paper and roll up jelly-roll fashion. Parmesan cheese will adhere to roulade. Place seam-side down on baking sheet. Arrange Cheddar cheese slices on top of roulade. Broil about 4 inches from heat until cheese just melts, about 3 minutes. Using 2 large spatulas, place roulade on a long narrow platter. Slice to serve. Makes 8 servings.

Spinach-Cheddar Filling:
In a medium skillet over medium heat, sauté onion in butter or margarine until soft but not browned. Add remaining ingredients. Remove from heat. Stir until blended.

Shred cheese just before measuring. It tends to pack down as it sits.

Creamy Chive Soufflé

Egg whites won't beat stiff if they contain even a trace of the yolk.

3 tablespoons butter or margarine
3 tablespoons all-purpose flour
1 teaspoon salt
1 cup milk
4 drops hot pepper sauce
1/2 (8-oz.) pkg. cream cheese, room
   temperature (4 oz.)

1/2 cup cream-style cottage cheese (4 oz.)
1 tablespoon snipped fresh parsley
1 tablespoon snipped fresh chives or
   freeze-dried chopped chives
6 eggs, separated

Melt butter or margarine in a medium saucepan over medium heat. Stir in flour and salt until mixture bubbles. Stir in milk and hot pepper sauce until mixture bubbles and thickens. Cook 1 minute longer. Stir in cream cheese, cottage cheese, parsley and chives. Remove from heat. Preheat oven to 350°F (175°C). In a large bowl, beat egg whites with electric mixer on high speed until stiff; set aside. In another large bowl, beat egg yolks until thick and pale. By hand, blend cheese mixture into beaten egg yolks. Fold in beaten egg whites until no streaks of white remain. Pour into an ungreased 8-cup soufflé dish or casserole dish with straight sides. With a rubber spatula, cut a shallow groove around top of soufflé mixture about 1 inch from edge. Bake about 45 minutes in preheated oven until soufflé is puffed, firm and golden. Serve immediately. Makes 6 to 8 servings.

Stovetop Cheese Soufflé

Unlike most other soufflés, this one will wait if dinner is delayed a little.

2 tablespoons butter or margarine
2 tablespoons all-purpose flour
1/2 teaspoon dry mustard
1/2 teaspoon salt

1 cup milk
1 cup shredded Swiss cheese (4 oz.)
4 eggs, separated

Melt butter or margarine in a medium saucepan over medium heat. Stir in flour, dry mustard and salt until mixture bubbles. Gradually stir in milk until sauce bubbles and thickens. Cook 1 minute longer. Stir in cheese until melted. Remove from heat. In a medium bowl, beat egg whites with electric mixer on high speed until soft peaks form; set aside. Beat egg yolks in a large bowl. Slowly beat cheese sauce into beaten egg yolks. Fold in beaten egg whites by hand until no streaks of white remain. Pour water 2 inches deep into bottom of double boiler. Turn egg mixture into top of double boiler; cover. Bring water to a boil. Turn down heat until water just simmers. Without lifting cover, cook soufflé over simmering water 1 hour. At the end of 1 hour, a knife inserted in center of soufflé should come out clean. If knife does not come out clean, cook 10 minutes longer. To serve, spoon onto individual dinner plates. Makes 4 servings.

Variation

Cheddar Stove-Top Soufflé: Substitute 3/4 teaspoon crumbled dried leaf oregano for the dry mustard. Substitute sharp Cheddar cheese for the Swiss cheese.

Calzone

Prosciutto or Italian ham is also delicious in sandwiches and omelets.

1 pkg. active dry yeast (1 tablespoon)
1 cup lukewarm water (about 105°F, 40°C)
4-1/2 cups all-purpose flour
2 tablespoons vegetable oil
1 teaspoon salt
1/8 teaspoon pepper
1/4 cup olive oil

1/2 lb. mozzarella cheese, slivered
1/4 lb. prosciutto ham, slivered
1/8 lb. salami sausage, slivered
1/2 teaspoon garlic salt
Water
1 tablespoon olive oil
2 tablespoons grated Romano cheese

Add yeast to lukewarm water. Stir to dissolve. Let stand 10 minutes. Measure flour into a large bowl. Make a well in the center. Pour yeast mixture and vegetable oil into well. Add salt and pepper. Work ingredients together with hands until combined. Turn dough out onto a lightly floured surface. Knead until dough is smooth and elastic, about 10 minutes. Clean and grease bowl. Place dough in bowl. Turn to grease all sides. Cover and let rise in a warm place free from drafts until doubled in bulk, about 2 hours. Preheat oven to 400°F (205°C). Punch down dough and divide into 6 equal pieces. Roll and stretch pieces of dough into six 4-inch circles, 1/4-inch thick. Brush circles evenly with 1/4 cup olive oil. Combine mozzarella cheese slivers, ham slivers, sausage slivers and garlic salt. Spread mixture evenly over half of each dough circle. Moisten edges with water. Fold dough over cheese mixture. Press edges with a fork that has been dipped in flour. Brush tops of calzone evenly with 1 tablespoon olive oil. Place on an ungreased baking sheet. Bake about 20 minutes in preheated oven until golden brown. Sprinkle immediately with Romano cheese. Serve hot. Makes 6 servings.

How to Make Dough for Calzone

1/Make a well in flour mixture. Add yeast mixture, oil, salt and pepper.

2/Combine ingredients with spoon or your hands until crumbs the size of large peas form.

Ready-to-Bake Swiss Soufflés

To bake without freezing, place in a 350°F (175°C) oven 35 to 40 minutes until puffed and golden.

2 tablespoons finely chopped shallots or
    green onions
6 tablespoons butter or margarine
6 tablespoons all-purpose flour
1/2 teaspoon salt
1-1/2 cups milk
1/2 teaspoon Dijon-style mustard

3 drops hot pepper sauce
1 cup shredded Swiss cheese (4 oz.)
6 eggs, separated
2 tablespoons snipped fresh parsley
1/4 teaspoon dried tarragon leaves, crumbled
1/4 teaspoon dried marjoram leaves, crumbled

Butter 6 freezer-to-oven 1 cup soufflé dishes or 10-ounce straight-sided ramekins; set aside. In a medium saucepan, sauté shallots or green onions in butter or margarine until limp but not browned, about 5 minutes. Stir in flour and salt until mixture bubbles. Gradually stir in milk until mixture bubbles and thickens. Stir in mustard and hot pepper sauce. Cook 2 minutes longer. Stir in cheese until melted. Remove from heat. Beat egg yolks in a small bowl. Stir 1/2 cup hot cheese mixture into beaten egg yolks. Stir egg yolk mixture into hot cheese mixture. Stir in parsley, tarragon and marjoram. In a large bowl, beat egg whites with electric mixer on high speed until stiff. By hand, fold cheese mixture into beaten egg whites. Spoon evenly into prepared soufflé dishes or ramekins. Wrap airtight in foil or freezer paper. Label, date and freeze. To serve frozen soufflés, preheat oven to 350°F (175°C). Remove soufflés from freezer. Unwrap and place on a baking sheet. Do not thaw. Bake about 45 minutes until puffed and golden. Makes 6 servings.

How to Make Ready-to-Bake Swiss Soufflés

1/Fold cooked Swiss cheese mixture into stiffly beaten egg whites.

2/Holding edges together, fold foil or freezer wrap tight. Roll sides of wrap down.

Frittata Italia

No matter what vegetable you change in this omelet, keep the onion for flavor.

2 tablespoons butter or margarine
1/2 cup chopped onion
1/2 cup chopped green pepper
1 large tomato, peeled, chopped
1/2 teaspoon salt
1/4 teaspoon dried oregano leaves, crumbled

8 eggs
1/2 teaspoon salt
1/8 teaspoon white pepper
2 tablespoons butter or margarine
1/2 cup shredded provolone cheese (2 oz.)

Melt 2 tablespoons butter or margarine in a small skillet over medium heat. Add onion and green pepper. Sauté until soft but not browned. Add tomato, 1/2 teaspoon salt and oregano. Simmer slowly until all liquid is absorbed, about 10 minutes. Stir occasionally; set aside. In a medium bowl, beat eggs lightly with 1/2 teaspoon salt and white pepper. In a 10-inch skillet, melt 2 tablespoons butter or margarine, tipping skillet to coat bottom and side. Pour in egg mixture. Shake skillet briskly back and forth over heat while stirring with the flat part of a fork until center begins to set. Finish cooking without stirring. Continued stirring will result in scrambled eggs. Omelet is done when firm on bottom and almost set on top. Spread sautéed onion mixture evenly over omelet. Sprinkle with cheese. Remove from heat. Cover skillet until cheese begins to melt, about 2 minutes. To serve, cut omelet into 4 equal pieces. Makes 4 servings.

Variation

Substitute shredded raw zucchini or carrot, chopped mushrooms or cooked vegetables such as broccoli or spinach for the green pepper and tomato. Always retain onion for flavor.

Dieter's Delight

This fondue is a treat for diabetic, low-calorie and low-fat dieters—and for nondieters too.

2 cups shredded low-fat American cheese
  (8 oz.)
1/2 cup low-fat milk or skim milk
1 tablespoon snipped fresh parsley
1 tablespoon grated onion
1 small garlic clove, minced
1 teaspoon dry mustard
1 teaspoon Worcestershire sauce

1/2 teaspoon dried dillweed, crushed
1/4 teaspoon celery seeds
1 cup broccoli flowerets
3 tablespoons water
1/2 teaspoon salt
1 cup zucchini slices, 1/4-inch thick
1 cup carrot slices, 1/4-inch thick
1 cup small fresh raw mushroom caps

Combine cheese, milk, parsley, onion, garlic, dry mustard, Worcestershire sauce, dillweed and celery seeds in a medium saucepan. Stir constantly over medium heat until cheese melts. Pour into a fondue pot or chafing dish. Keep warm over a low flame. Place broccoli flowerets, water and salt in a small saucepan with a tight lid. Cover and simmer over medium heat until crisp-tender, about 15 minutes; drain. To serve, place hot cooked broccoli flowerets, zucchini slices, carrot slices and mushroom caps in individual serving dishes. Using forks, dip vegetables into fondue. Makes 4 servings.

Easy Chocolate Soufflé

Your blender does all the work!

1-1/2 cups semisweet chocolate
  flavored pieces
1 cup heavy cream or whipping cream
5 eggs
1 (8-oz.) pkg. cream cheese,
  cut into 4 equal pieces

1 tablespoon vanilla extract, 1 tablespoon
  dark rum or 2 tablespoons orange-
  flavored liqueur
1/8 teaspoon salt
Whipped cream, if desired

Preheat oven to 375°F (190°C). Grease a 1-1/2-quart soufflé dish or deep casserole dish with straight sides; set aside. Place chocolate pieces in blender. In a small saucepan, bring cream to boiling point. Do not boil. Start blender at medium speed. Slowly pour in hot cream. Blend 1 minute. Continue to blend, adding eggs 1 at a time. Add cream cheese, vanilla, rum or liqueur and salt. Blend until combined. Pour into prepared dish. Bake 1 hour in preheated oven. Serve immediately with whipped cream, if desired. Makes 6 servings.

Costa Rican Flan

Cream of coconut is displayed with fruit juices or liquor mixes in most supermarkets.

2 cups sugar
2 cups light corn syrup
1 tablespoon butter
1 cup freshly grated Parmesan cheese (3 oz.)
1 (8.5-oz.) can cream of coconut
6 tablespoons all-purpose flour

1 whole egg
8 egg yolks
1 cup heavy cream or whipping cream,
  whipped
1/2 cup toasted slivered almonds

Generously grease a 1-1/2 quart casserole; set aside. Stir sugar and syrup in a medium saucepan to combine. Attach a candy thermometer to side of pan. Without stirring, simmer over low heat until mixture reaches 300°F (150°C) on thermometer. Mixture will be a light caramel color and separate into brittle threads when dropped from a spoon into water. Remove from heat. Stir in butter until melted. Blend Parmesan cheese into syrup mixture until melted. Preheat oven to 350°F (175°C). In a small bowl, combine cream of coconut and flour to make a smooth paste. Stir into syrup until blended. In the same small bowl, beat whole egg and egg yolks. Stir 1/2 cup of the syrup mixture into eggs. Stirring vigorously, slowly pour egg mixture into syrup mixture until blended. Pour into prepared casserole. Place casserole in a slightly larger baking dish. Pour water 1 to 1-1/2 inches deep into outer dish. Bake about 40 minutes in preheated oven until a knife inserted in center comes out clean. Cool slightly. Refrigerate until cold, about 1 hour. To serve, invert casserole onto a platter; remove casserole. Spoon dollops of whipped cream on top of flan. Make peaks by pulling cream upward with the back of a metal spoon. Sprinkle with slivered almonds. Makes 8 to 10 servings.

Variation

Substitute 2 cups crushed, sweetened strawberries, raspberries or blackberries for whipped cream.

Tarte à l'Orange

Work quickly or the filling will set before you get it into the crust.

Sweetened Crumb Crust made with
   graham cracker crumbs, page 129
1/3 cup Grand Marnier
1-1/2 teaspoons unflavored gelatin powder
2 eggs, separated
1/8 teaspoon cream of tartar
2 tablespoons sugar
3/4 cup plus 2 tablespoons heavy cream or
   whipping cream

1 (8-oz.) pkg. cream cheese, room temperature
2 teaspoons grated lemon peel
2 tablespoons grated orange peel
3 tablespoons sugar
1/2 cup heavy cream or whipping cream
6 candied cherries, halved
10 strips candied orange peel

Prepare and bake Sweetened Crumb Crust in a 10-inch tart pan or pie pan. Cool on a rack. Pour Grand Marnier into a small saucepan. Stir in gelatin powder. Let stand 10 minutes. In a small bowl, beat egg whites with electric mixer on medium speed until frothy. On high speed, beat in cream of tartar until soft peaks form. Gradually beat in 2 tablespoons sugar until high stiff peaks form; set aside. With same beaters, beat 3/4 cup plus 2 tablespoons cream until stiff; refrigerate. In a small bowl, beat cream cheese until fluffy. Beat in lemon peel, orange peel and 3 tablespoons sugar. Beat in egg yolks 1 at a time until blended; set aside. Stir Grand Marnier and gelatin powder over low heat until gelatin is completely dissolved. Do not boil. Stir gelatin mixture into cream cheese mixture until just blended. Quickly stir in 1 heaping tablespoonful of the whipped cream until no white remains. Fold in remaining whipped cream. Quickly but gently fold in beaten egg whites. Immediately pour into cooled crust. Refrigerate 2 hours or overnight. To serve, whip 1/2 cup cream until stiff. Spoon dollops of the whipped cream around edge of tart. Decorate whipped cream dollops with candied cherry halves and candied orange peel strips. Makes 8 to 10 servings.

Tyrolean Rice Pudding

Don't use converted or partially cooked rice in this recipe. It is too soft.

1 cup long-grain white rice, uncooked
1/4 cup butter or margarine
1 qt. milk
1/2 cup sugar
1 tablespoon vanilla extract
1 cup shredded Swiss cheese (4 oz.)

2 cooking apples
4 eggs
1/4 cup sugar
1 teaspoon ground cinnamon or
   1/2 teaspoon ground nutmeg

Combine rice, butter or margarine, milk and 1/2 cup sugar in a medium saucepan over medium heat. Bring to boiling point; do not boil. Reduce heat. Stirring occasionally, simmer until rice is tender, 20 to 25 minutes. Stir in vanilla and cheese until cheese melts. Let stand 15 minutes. Peel, core and slice apples; set aside. Preheat oven to 350°F (175°C). Grease a 9" x 9" baking dish; set aside. Beat eggs 1 at a time into cooled rice mixture until blended. Pour into prepared baking dish. Arrange apple slices on rice mixture like spokes of a wheel. Sprinkle with 1/4 cup sugar and cinnamon or nutmeg. Bake 30 minutes in preheated oven. Serve warm or cold. Makes 6 to 8 servings.

Great Blueberry Swirl

Your ice cream maker never turned out anything more delicious!

Blueberry Deco, see below
2 egg yolks
1/2 cup sugar
1 cup half-and-half or light cream
2 (8-oz.) pkgs. Neufchâtel cheese
1/2 cup sugar

1/2 teaspoon grated lemon peel
1/2 teaspoon grated orange peel
1 tablespoon lemon juice
1/2 teaspoon vanilla extract
1 pint plain yogurt

Blueberry Deco:
1/2 cup water
1/4 cup sugar
1 teaspoon cornstarch

1 tablespoon lemon juice
1 cup fresh or frozen unsweetened blueberries
1/8 teaspoon ground cinnamon

Prepare Blueberry Deco. In a heavy saucepan, beat egg yolks and 1/2 cup sugar until blended. Beat in cream. Stir constantly over low heat until custard coats a metal spoon. Do not boil. Remove from heat. Place waxed paper or plastic wrap directly on surface of custard. Refrigerate to chill, about 2 hours. In a large bowl, beat cheese until fluffy. Add 1/2 cup sugar, lemon peel, orange peel, lemon juice and vanilla. Beat until blended. Beat in yogurt and chilled custard until smooth. Freeze in ice cream maker following manufacturer's directions. When mixture stops churning, remove metal ice cream container from bucket. Use a long-handled wooden spoon to swirl chilled Blueberry Deco into frozen mixture to create a marbled effect. Cover ice cream container. Place in freezer until firm, about 3 hours. Makes about 2 quarts.

Blueberry Deco:
Combine water and sugar in a medium saucepan. Bring to a boil, stirring to dissolve sugar. Stir cornstarch into lemon juice until smooth. Stir cornstarch mixture into sugar mixture until thickened. Add blueberries and cinnamon. Boil 2 minutes, mashing berries slightly with the back of a spoon. Remove from heat. Refrigerate to chill about 2 hours.

How To Make Breadcrumbs

Fine Dry Breadcrumbs: Spread 6 bread slices in a single layer on a baking sheet. Bake at 300°F (150°C) until completely dry and lightly browned, about 30 minutes, turning once. Process dried bread a little at a time in blender until crumbs form. Sieve and reprocess if necessary. Makes about I cup.
Soft Breadcrumbs: Remove crusts from 3 slices of day-old bread. Tear bread into large pieces and process a few at a time in blender until crumbs form. Makes 3/4 to 1 cup.
Soft Buttered Breadcrumbs: Butter 3 slices of day-old bread. Follow directions for Soft Breadcrumbs. Makes 3/4 to 1 cup.

Baking

Yeast is a friendly living organism. You and yeast can make beautiful breads together if you approach baking with confidence. Here are some phrases used in yeast bread recipes which may be new to you or which may be useful as a review.

Warm Water—If you don't have a thermometer, test the water by placing a few drops on the inside of your wrist. *Lukewarm* (about 105°F, 40°C) feels neutral—neither warm nor cool. *Warm* (about 110°F, 45°C) feels just warm. *Very warm* (about 125°F, 50°C) is considerably warmer, but doesn't burn.

Cover With a Cloth—The cloth may be dry or wet, according to the recipe. A wet cloth adds moisture to the dough.

Warm Place, Free from Drafts—Put the covered bowl containing the dough on the top shelf of your oven. Put a large flat pan filled with hot water on the bottom shelf.

Doubled in Bulk—Mark the outside of the bowl with a piece of masking tape if necessary. Or press the center top of the dough with two fingers. If the dough springs back most of the way, let it rise 15 to 20 minutes longer. If the indentation remains, the dough has doubled in bulk.

Let Dough Rest—Means what it says. Cover the dough, then ignore it for the specified time.

Punch Down Dough—Go ahead—whack it with your fist! Bread doughs are remarkably sturdy. If you prefer to be gentle, press down the center of the dough with your fist, then pull the sides of the dough toward the center.

Knead—Place the dough on a lightly floured surface. With lightly floured hands, pick up the dough edge on the side away from you. Fold it toward you. Press down on the dough firmly with the heels of your hands while gently pushing away from you. Turn the dough 1/4 turn. Again pick up the dough on the side away from you, fold it over and press down firmly while pushing away from you. Repeat this action for about 10 minutes until the dough is smooth and elastic.

If you are a novice baker, the first rule to learn is **don't be intimidated!** Read the recipe all the way through, assemble all ingredients, measure carefully and follow directions exactly.

Ranch Supper
Texas Chili
Panhandle Cornbread, page 112
Carrot & Celery Slaw
Sliced Oranges with Sour Cream
Cottage Jumbles, page 120

Pictured on the following pages. Clockwise from top center: Holiday Cheddar Date Cake, page 115; Polka Dot Quick Bread, page 125; French Gruyere Braid, page 112.

French Gruyère Braids *Photo on page 110.*

It takes less time and effort to mix breads if you use your mixer.

1 cup very warm water (about 125°F, 50°C)	4 eggs, room temperature
1 pkg. active dry yeast (1 tablespoon)	6 oz. Gruyère cheese, diced
3-1/2 to 4-1/2 cups all-purpose flour	1 egg
1 teaspoon sugar	1 tablespoon milk
1-1/2 teaspoons salt	2 tablespoons celery seeds
3/4 cup butter or margarine, room temperature	

Pour warm water into a warm large bowl. Add yeast. Stir to dissolve. Let stand until light and puffed, about 5 minutes. Add 1-1/2 cups flour, sugar and salt. Beat with electric mixer on lowest speed 1 minute. Beat on medium speed 2 minutes longer. Add butter or margarine to yeast mixture. Beat 1 minute longer. On lowest speed, beat in 1 egg and 1/2 cup of the flour, repeating until 4 eggs are used and enough of the flour to make a soft, sticky dough. Continue to beat with mixer or by hand until dough is glossy and elastic and pulls away from side of bowl. Stir in cheese by hand. Cover and let rise in a warm place free from drafts until doubled in bulk, 2-1/2 to 3 hours. When dough has doubled in bulk, place in refrigerator 5 hours or overnight. Remove from refrigerator. Divide dough in half. Cover and refrigerate half of the dough. Knead second half on a lightly floured surface until soft and pliable. Divide dough into 3 equal parts. With hands, roll each piece into a rope 12 to 16 inches long. Braid ropes, starting in the middle and working toward each end. Pinch ends to seal. Grease a large baking sheet. Place braid on one side of a prepared baking sheet. Repeat with refrigerated half of dough. In a small bowl, beat 1 egg and milk. Brush braids with egg mixture. Let braids rise in a warm place free from drafts until doubled in bulk, 1-1/2 to 2 hours. Do not cover. Midway through rising time, brush again with egg mixture. Preheat oven to 400°F (205°C). Again brush braids with egg mixture. Sprinkle evenly with celery seeds. Bake 40 minutes in pre-heated oven until a wooden skewer or pick inserted in braid comes out dry. Remove from baking sheet. Cool on racks. Makes 2 braids.

Panhandle Corn Bread

Serve this delicious loaf for breakfast or with Chicken Monterey, page 72.

1 cup yellow cornmeal	1/2 cup vegetable oil
1 tablespoon baking powder	1 cup dairy sour cream
1 cup shredded sharp Cheddar cheese (4 oz.)	1 (8-oz.) can cream-style corn
2 eggs, slightly beaten	1 (4-oz.) can chopped green chile peppers

Preheat oven to 400°F (205°C). Generously grease a 12-cup bundt or 9-inch tube pan; set aside. In a large bowl, combine cornmeal and baking powder. Stir in cheese. In a medium bowl, beat eggs, oil, sour cream, corn and chiles. Add to cornmeal mixture. Stir until just moistened. Spoon into prepared pan. Bake 40 to 50 minutes in preheated oven until wooden pick inserted in center comes out clean. Cool on a rack 10 minutes. Invert onto a serving plate. Makes 1 loaf.

Hearthside Cheddar Bread

Quick-breads should be stirred only until the moisture is distributed. Overmixing causes tunnels.

2-1/2 cups all-purpose flour
1/2 cup sugar
2 teaspoons baking powder
1 teaspoon salt
1/2 teaspoon ground cinnamon
3/4 cup milk

1/4 cup vegetable oil
2 eggs
1-1/2 cups chopped peeled cooking apples
2 cups shredded sharp Cheddar cheese (8 oz.)
3/4 cup chopped walnuts or pecans

Preheat oven to 350°F (175°C). Grease and flour a 9" x 5" loaf pan; set aside. In a large bowl, combine flour, sugar, baking powder, salt and cinnamon. Make a well in the center. Add milk, oil and eggs. Stir until thoroughly combined. Gently stir in apples, cheese and nuts. Spoon into prepared pan. Bake 1 hour and 15 minutes in preheated oven until loaf is browned and sounds hollow when tapped on bottom. Cool in pan on a rack 5 minutes. Remove from pan. Cool to room temperature on rack before slicing. Makes 1 loaf.

Hausfrau's Pleasure

Bierkäse or beer cheese *is similar to* limburger. *Use* Swiss *cheese for a milder flavor.*

2-1/2 cups warm water (about 110°F, 45°C)
1 pkg. active dry yeast (1 tablespoon)
8 cups all-purpose flour
2 cups shredded bierkäse cheese (8 oz.)
1 cup mashed potatoes, without butter or salt

1/4 cup finely snipped fresh dill or
   2 tablespoons crushed dried dillweed
1-1/2 tablespoons salt
1 egg
1 tablespoon cold water

Pour 1/2 cup of the warm water into a warm large bowl. Add yeast. Stir gently to dissolve. Stir in 3 tablespoons of the flour. Cover; let stand until bubbly, about 30 minutes. Stir in remaining 2 cups warm water. Add all of the remaining flour, cheese, potatoes, dill and salt. Mix until a stiff dough forms. Use hands if necessary. Turn out onto a lightly floured surface. Let dough rest 8 to 10 minutes. Clean and grease bowl; set aside. Knead dough until smooth and elastic, about 10 minutes. Place dough in prepared bowl. Turn to grease all sides. Cover and let rise in a warm place free from drafts until doubled in bulk, about 2 hours. Grease 2 baking sheets; set aside. Divide dough in half. Shape each half into a round ball. Place on prepared baking sheets. Cover and let rise in a warm place free from drafts until doubled in bulk, 30 to 40 minutes. Preheat oven to 400°F (205°C). With a sharp knife make several lengthwise and crosswise cuts on tops of loaves. In a small bowl, lightly beat egg and 1 tablespoon cold water. Gently brush tops of loaves with egg mixture. Bake 45 minutes in preheated oven until loaves sound hollow when tapped on bottom. Remove at once from baking sheets. Cool on racks. Makes 2 loaves.

Yeast is sensitive to temperature changes. If a cold breeze blows across your yeast dough, it can kill the yeast and keep the dough from rising.

Cheese-Onion Pinwheels

When you roll out dough, start in the middle and roll toward the edge.

1/3 cup sugar	1/2 cup butter or margarine
1 teaspoon salt	3 eggs
2 pkgs. active dry yeast (2 tablespoons)	3 cups shredded sharp Cheddar cheese (12 oz.)
About 6 cups all-purpose flour	1 cup finely chopped onion
1-1/4 cups milk	Paprika

Combine sugar, salt, yeast and 2 cups of the flour in a large bowl; set aside. In a small saucepan, heat milk and butter or margarine until very warm, about 125°F (50°C). Slowly stir hot milk mixture into flour mixture. Add eggs. Beat 2 minutes by hand or with electric mixer on medium speed, scraping bowl occasionally. Stir in enough of the remaining flour by hand to make a stiff dough. Turn out onto a lightly floured surface. Let rest 8 to 10 minutes. Clean and grease bowl; set aside. Knead dough until smooth and elastic, 8 to 10 minutes. Place dough in bowl. Turn to grease all sides. Cover with a dry cloth towel. Let rise in a warm place free from drafts until doubled in bulk, about 1 hour. Grease 2 baking sheets; set aside. Press down center of dough with 2 fingers. If indentations remain, punch down dough. Divide in half. On a lightly floured surface, roll out each half of dough to an 18" x 10" rectangle. Sprinkle each with half of the cheese and half of the onion. Roll up from long side jelly-roll fashion. Place 1 rolled loaf on each prepared baking sheet, seam-side down. Curve loaves slightly. With a sharp knife, cut 1/2-inch deep gashes about 1 inch apart across top of each loaf. Cover with towel. Let rise in a warm place free from drafts until doubled in bulk, about 45 minutes. Preheat oven to 350°F (175°C). Sprinkle tops of loaves with paprika. Bake 25 to 30 minutes in preheated oven until loaves sound hollow when tapped on top. Cool to room temperature on racks. Makes 2 loaves.

How to Make Cheese-Onion Pinwheels

1/Press down dough with 2 fingers. If indentation remains, punch down dough.

Holiday Cheddar Date Cake *Photo on page 110.*

Make this flavorful fruitcake well in advance so it will have time to mellow.

3/4 cup butter or margarine,
   room temperature
1-1/2 cups firmly packed light brown sugar
4 eggs
1 cup shredded sharp Cheddar cheese (4 oz.)
3-1/2 cups all-purpose flour
1/2 teaspoon baking soda
1 teaspoon salt
1 teaspoon ground cinnamon

1/4 teaspoon ground cloves
2 (8-oz.) pkgs. pitted dates, finely chopped
2 cups chopped pecans
1 (4-oz.) jar red candied cherries, halved
2 cups golden raisins
1 cup milk
4 slices candied pineapple, quartered,
   if desired
12 whole blanched almonds, if desired

Preheat oven to 300°F (150°C). Grease and flour a 10-inch tube pan; set aside. In a large bowl, beat butter or margarine and brown sugar with electric mixer on medium speed until blended. Add eggs one at a time, beating well after each addition. Beat in cheese. Sift flour, baking soda, salt, cinnamon and cloves into a medium bowl. In another medium bowl, combine dates, pecans, cherries and raisins. Add 2 tablespoons of the flour mixture, tossing lightly to coat fruit and nuts. Alternately beat remaining flour mixture and milk into butter mixture until blended. Stir in floured fruit mixture by hand until distributed throughout batter. Turn into prepared pan. Bake 2 to 2-1/2 hours in preheated oven until cake shrinks from side of pan and top springs back when lightly pressed. Cool 15 minutes on a rack. Remove from pan. If desired, decorate top with pineapple pieces and whole almonds. When cool, store in a container with a tight lid up to 6 weeks. To serve, cut into thin slices. Makes 20 to 24 servings.

2/Sprinkle cheese and onion over rectangles of dough. Roll up jelly-roll fashion.

3/With seam-sides down, make 1/2-inch-deep cuts 1 inch apart across top of loaves.

Merlin's Magic Cupcakes

Some of the topping sinks, making a luscious creamy filling.

Chipper Filling, see below
6 tablespoons finely chopped pecans
1-1/2 cups all-purpose flour
1 cup sugar
1/4 cup unsweetened cocoa powder
1 teaspoon baking soda

1/2 teaspoon salt
1 cup water
5 tablespoons vegetable oil
1 tablespoon cider vinegar
1 teaspoon vanilla extract

Chipper Filling:
1 (8-oz.) pkg. cream cheese, room
   temperature
1 egg

1/3 cup sugar
1 (6-oz.) pkg. semisweet chocolate pieces

Prepare Chipper Filling; set aside. Preheat oven to 350°F (175°C). Place paper liners in 18 muffin cups. Sprinkle 1 teaspoon pecans into each cup; set aside. In a large bowl, combine flour, sugar, cocoa powder, baking soda and salt. In a medium bowl, beat water, oil, vinegar and vanilla. Gradually stir water mixture into flour mixture until blended. Carefully spoon batter into prepared baking cups, filling about half full. Top each with 1 tablespoon Chipper Filling. Bake 25 minutes in preheated oven until top springs back when gently pressed. Cool on a rack 5 minutes. Invert onto rack. Remove muffin pan and paper liners. Serve at room temperature. Makes 18 cup cakes.

Chipper Filling:
In a medium bowl, beat cream cheese, egg and sugar until smooth. Stir in chocolate pieces.

Butterscotch-Cream Squares

Keep these cookies in your refrigerator.

1/2 cup firmly packed light brown sugar
1/4 cup butter or margarine,
   room temperature
1 cup biscuit mix
1/2 cup chopped walnuts
1 (8-oz.) pkg. cream cheese,
   room temperature

1/4 cup granulated sugar
1 tablespoon lemon juice
2 teaspoons milk
1/2 teaspoon vanilla extract
1 egg

Preheat oven to 350°F (175°C). Grease an 8" x 8" baking dish; set aside. In a medium bowl, beat brown sugar and butter or margarine until fluffy. Stir in biscuit mix and walnuts until mixture is crumbly. Reserve 1 cup. Press remaining crumb mixture into prepared baking dish. Bake 12 minutes in preheated oven. In a medium bowl, stir cream cheese and granulated sugar until blended. Beat in lemon juice, milk, vanilla extract and egg until mixture is smooth. Spread cream cheese mixture evenly over hot baked layer. Sprinkle with reserved crumb mixture. Bake about 25 minutes until center is firm. Cool on a rack. Cut into 2-inch squares. Refrigerate until served. Makes 16 squares.

Marbled Marvels

These chocolate bars with a delectable cheese filling put plain brownies to shame.

1 cup butter or margarine	1/2 teaspoon salt
4 (1-oz.) squares unsweetened baking chocolate	1 teaspoon vanilla extract
2 cups sugar	1 (8-oz.) pkg. cream cheese, room temperature
2 eggs	1/2 cup sugar
1 cup all-purpose flour	1 egg
1 cup chopped walnuts	1 teaspoon vanilla extract

Preheat oven to 350°F (175°C). Grease a 13" x 9" baking dish; set aside. Melt butter or margarine and chocolate in a heavy 3-quart saucepan over low heat. Remove from heat. Beat in 2 cups sugar and 2 eggs until blended. Stir in flour, nuts, salt and 1 teaspoon vanilla. Spread evenly in prepared baking dish. In a small bowl, beat cream cheese, 1/2 cup sugar, 1 egg and 1 teaspoon vanilla by hand or with electric mixer on low speed until blended. Beat 2 minutes longer on medium speed, scraping bowl often. Drop cheese mixture onto chocolate mixture by teaspoonfuls. With the tip of a knife, gently cut through cheese layer and into top of chocolate layer in a criss-cross pattern to give a marbled effect. Bake 40 to 45 minutes in preheated oven until a wooden pick inserted in center comes out clean. Cool on a rack. Cut into 3" x 2" bars. Refrigerate until served. Makes 18 bars.

Perfection Pound Cake

You can mix this cake by hand, but it will take more effort to get the same results.

1 (8-oz.) pkg. cream cheese, room temperature	4 eggs
3/4 cup butter or margarine, room temperature	2 cups sifted cake flour
	1-1/4 teaspoons baking powder
1-1/2 cups granulated sugar	1 teaspoon ground mace
	Powdered sugar, if desired

Preheat oven to 325°F (165°C). Butter and flour a 9" x 5" loaf pan; set aside. Blend cream cheese, butter or margarine and granulated sugar in a large bowl with electric mixer on medium speed. On low speed, beat in eggs until blended. Sift cake flour, baking powder and mace into a small bowl. Gradually beat flour mixture into cheese mixture until smooth. Pour into prepared pan. Bake 1 hour 20 minutes in preheated oven until golden brown and surface springs back when gently touched. Cool on a rack 5 minutes. Remove from pan. Cool to room temperature on rack. Sprinkle with powdered sugar if desired. Makes 12 to 14 servings.

Variations

Omit mace if desired. Add 1-1/2 teaspoons vanilla extract, 1 teaspoon lemon extract or 1/2 teaspoon almond extract. Frost with one of the cream cheese frostings on page 126.

Peach Dumplings

Hot topping causes the cream cheese to melt deliciously over the dumplings.

1 (29-oz.) can peach halves
1-1/2 cups all-purpose flour
3/4 teaspoon salt
1/2 cup vegetable shortening
1/2 cup shredded sharp Cheddar cheese
  (2 oz.)

3 to 4 tablespoons cold water
2 tablespoons butter or margarine
Ground cinnamon
Peach Topping, see below
1 (8-oz.) pkg. cream cheese,
  room temperature

Peach Topping:

1/4 cup sugar
1 tablespoon cornstarch
1 cup reserved peach syrup

1 teaspoon shredded lemon peel
1 teaspoon lemon juice
1 tablespoon butter or margarine

Preheat oven to 425°F (220°C). Drain peach halves, reserving 1 cup syrup for topping. Set aside. Blend flour and salt in a medium bowl. Cut in shortening with a pastry blender or 2 knives until mixture is the size of small peas. Stir in Cheddar cheese. Toss gently wth a fork while adding water 1 tablespoon at a time. Toss until moisture is distributed. Shape dough into a ball. On a lightly floured surface, roll out dough to an 18" x 12" rectangle. Use a knife or pastry cutter to cut dough in half to make two 18" x 6" strips. Cut each strip into three 6-inch squares. Place 1 peach half cut-side down in the center of each square. Cut butter or margarine into small pieces. Distribute evenly over peaches. Sprinkle lightly with cinnamon. Moisten edges of pastry with water. Bring corners together over peach halves. Pinch corners and edges together to make a tight seal. Place on an un-greased baking sheet. Bake 20 to 25 minutes in preheated oven until golden brown. While dumplings bake, prepare Peach Topping. Cut cream cheese into 6 equal pieces. Place baked dumplings in small dessert dishes. Top each dumpling with a piece of cream cheese. Spoon hot topping evenly over dumplings and cheese. Serve immediately. Makes 6 servings.

Peach Topping:

Blend sugar and cornstarch in a small saucepan. Place over medium heat. Gradually stir in reserved peach syrup until thickened and bubbly. Stir in lemon peel, lemon juice and butter or margarine until smooth. Keep warm over low heat.

It's easy to cut cake layers in half. Place food picks at the cutting line and saw through the cake layer with a serrated knife or a strong linen thread, using the food picks as a guide.

Easy-Do Swiss Torte

Powdered sugar usually needs to be sifted to get rid of lumps.

1 (18-1/2-oz.) pkg. devil's food cake mix	1 cup half-and-half or light cream
Water	1 cup dairy sour cream
2 eggs	1-1/2 cups shredded Gruyère cheese (6 oz.)
2 tablespoons grated orange peel	2 teaspoons vanilla extract
3 tablespoons cornstarch	1 tablespoon powdered sugar
1/3 cup granulated sugar	

Preheat oven to 350°F (175°C). Grease and flour two 9-inch, round cake pans. Prepare cake mix with water and eggs according to package directions. Stir in orange peel. Bake as directed in preheated oven. Turn baked cake layers out of pans onto racks. Combine cornstarch and granulated sugar in a medium saucepan. Gradually stir in half-and-half or light cream and sour cream. Stir constantly over low heat until mixture bubbles and thickens. Add cheese 1/2 cup at a time, stirring after each addition until smooth. Remove from heat. Cool 15 minutes. Stir in vanilla. Refrigerate until mixture has thickened, about 2 hours. Cut each cake layer in half, making 4 thin layers. Place 1 layer on a serving dish. Spread with 1/3 of the cheese filling. Repeat twice. Top with remaining cake layer. Sift powdered sugar over top of torte. Makes 10 to 12 servings.

How to Make Peach Dumplings

1/Cut dough into six 6-inch squares. Place 1 peach half, cut-side down, in center of each square.

2/Bring corners together over peach halves. Pinch corners and edges together to make a tight seal.

Celebration Cake

Coating fruits and nuts with flour helps to keep them from sinking as the cake bakes.

1/2 cup finely chopped pecans	1-1/2 teaspoons baking powder
1 (8-oz.) pkg. cream cheese, room temperature	4 eggs
	1 cup mixed diced candied fruit
1 cup butter or margarine, room temperature	1/2 cup chopped blanched almonds
	1/4 cup sifted cake flour
1-1/2 cups sugar	6 candied red cherries, halved
1-1/2 teaspoons vanilla extract	12 whole blanched almonds
2 cups sifted cake flour	

Butter a 10-inch tube pan. Sprinkle with finely chopped pecans; set aside. Preheat oven to 325°F (165°C). In a large bowl, combine cream cheese, butter or margarine, sugar and vanilla. Beat with electric mixer on medium speed until blended. Sift 2 cups cake flour and baking powder into a small bowl. Gradually beat into cheese mixture. Add eggs one at a time beating well after each addition. In a small bowl, combine fruit, chopped almonds and 1/4 cup flour. Toss to coat fruits and nuts. Fold into batter by hand. Carefully pour batter into prepared pan. Bake 1 hour 20 minutes in preheated oven until cake shrinks slightly from side of pan and surface springs back when touched. Cool on a rack 10 minutes. Remove from pan. Decorate top with cherries and almonds. Cool to room temperature. Wrap airtight with plastic wrap or foil and store at room temperature. To serve, cut into thin slices. Makes 18 to 20 servings.

Cottage Jumbles

Unprocessed bran or miller's bran *is available in many supermarkets and health food stores.*

1/4 cup toasted wheat germ	1/4 cup butter or margarine, room temperature
1 cup whole-wheat flour	
1/4 cup unprocessed bran	1/2 cup cream-style cottage cheese (4 oz.)
1/4 cup nonfat dry milk powder	1/2 cup sugar
2 teaspoons baking powder	1/4 cup honey
1 teaspoon ground cinnamon	1 egg
1/4 teaspoon ground nutmeg	1 teaspoon vanilla extract
1/2 teaspoon salt	

Preheat oven to 350°F (175°C). Grease 2 large baking sheets; set aside. If toasted wheat germ is not available, bake untoasted wheat germ 10 minutes in a 375°F (190°C) oven. Combine toasted wheat germ, flour, bran, dry milk, baking powder, cinnamon, nutmeg and salt in a medium bowl; set aside. In a large bowl, beat butter or margarine and cottage cheese by hand or with electric mixer on medium speed until creamy and smooth. Beat in sugar, honey, egg and vanilla until fluffy. Gradually stir in flour mixture by hand until thoroughly combined. Drop by rounded teaspoonfuls about 2 inches apart on prepared baking sheets. Bake 8 to 10 minutes in preheated oven until golden brown around edges. Place on racks to cool. Makes about 30 cookies.

Tarte Tatin au Fromage *Photo on pages 122 and 123.*

You'll need 7 ounces of Gruyère cheese for this delicious upside-down treat.

3/4 cup sugar
5 large cooking apples
2 tablespoons brandy or apple juice
9 tablespoons sugar

1/4 cup butter or margarine
Gruyère Pastry, see below
3/4 cup shredded Gruyère cheese (3 oz.)

Gruyère Pastry:
1-1/2 cups all-purpose flour
1 cup shredded Gruyère cheese (4 oz.)
1 egg
1/4 teaspoon salt

3 tablespoons butter, room temperature
1/4 cup cold water
Grated peel of 1 lemon
 (about 1-1/2 teaspoons)

Place 3/4 cup sugar in a heavy skillet. Stir occasionally over medium heat until sugar melts and turns golden brown. Carefully pour into a 10-inch round pan with straight sides, 1-1/2 to 2 inches deep. Tilt pan to spread evenly. Peel and core apples. Slice 1/2-inch thick. Overlap apple slices on top of caramelized sugar, making 3 layers. Sprinkle each layer with 2 teaspoons of the brandy or apple juice and 3 tablespoons of the sugar. Dot apples with butter or margarine. Preheat oven to 350°F (175°C). Prepare Gruyère Pastry. Center over apples. Bake 40 to 45 minutes in preheated oven until crust is browned and apples are tender. Invert onto a large round platter. Sprinkle with 3/4 cup shredded Gruyère cheese. Cut into wedges and serve warm. Makes 8 to 10 servings.

Gruyère Pastry:
Toss flour and cheese in a medium bowl. Make a well in center. Place remaining ingredients in well. Mix with a fork until blended. Knead about 8 times, forming a smooth ball. On a lightly floured surface, roll out dough to a 10-inch circle.

Sunrise Popovers

These are high, golden, meltingly tender and easy to make. What more could you ask?

4 tablespoons vegetable shortening
1-1/3 cups all-purpose flour
1/2 teaspoon salt
2/3 cup milk

2/3 cup water
4 eggs
1/2 cup shredded sharp Cheddar cheese
 (2 oz.)

Preheat oven to 375°F (190°C). Place eight 6-ounce custard cups on a large baking sheet. Spoon 1-1/2 teaspoons shortening into bottom of each custard cup; set aside. Combine flour and salt in a large bowl. Gradually stir in milk and water until blended. Beat in eggs 1 at a time until mixture is smooth. Fold in cheese. Place baking sheet with custard cups in preheated oven 3 to 5 minutes until shortening melts and custard cups are hot. Fill custard cups 1/2 to 2/3 full with batter. Bake 45 minutes in preheated oven without opening door until popovers rise and turn golden brown. If not golden brown after 45 minutes, bake 5 minutes longer. Serve immediately. Makes 8 servings.

Tarte Tatin au Fromage is pictured on the following pages.

Company Brunch Babkas

Adding a little sugar to the yeast mixture speeds up the activity of the yeast.

1 pkg. active dry yeast (1 tablespoon)
1/4 cup granulated sugar
1/4 cup very warm water
   (about 125°F, 50°C)
3-1/2 to 4 cups all-purpose flour
3/4 teaspoon salt
2 teaspoons grated lemon peel
2 egg yolks

2 whole eggs
1/3 cup warm milk (about 110°F, 45°C)
6 tablespoons butter or margarine,
   room temperature
Lemon-Cheese Filling, see below
Nut Topping, see below
Powdered sugar

Lemon-Cheese Filling:

1 (8-oz.) pkg. cream cheese,
   room temperature
1/2 cup cream-style cottage cheese (4 oz.)

1 egg yolk
1/4 cup sugar
1 teaspoon grated lemon peel

Nut Topping:

1/3 cup chopped walnuts
3 tablespoons all-purpose flour
3 tablespoons butter or margarine,
   room temperature

3 tablespoons sugar
1/4 teaspoon ground cinnamon

Dissolve yeast and 1/2 teaspoon granulated sugar in water. Let stand 10 minutes until bubbly. Combine 2 cups flour, salt, lemon peel and remaining granulated sugar in a large bowl. Make a well in the center. In a small bowl, lightly beat egg yolks and whole eggs. Pour beaten eggs, yeast mixture and milk into well. Gradually combine. Beat well. Add butter or margarine a little at a time, beating well after each addition. Stir in 1 to 1-1/2 cups flour until dough leaves side of bowl. Turn out on a lightly floured surface. Let dough rest 8 to 10 minutes. Clean and grease bowl; set aside. Knead dough 10 minutes until smooth and elastic. Place dough in prepared bowl. Turn to grease all sides. Cover. Let rise in a warm place until doubled in bulk, 1-1/2 to 2 hours. Prepare Lemon-Cheese Filling and Nut Topping; set aside. Grease two 8-inch, round cake pans; set aside. Punch down dough. Divide into 4 equal parts. With floured hands, press 1 part over bottom and about 1/2 inch up the side of the pan. Repeat with second portion. Spread filling evenly over dough. Shape remaining dough into two 8-inch circles. Place over fillings. Press edges with the handle of a wooden spoon to seal. Sprinkle topping over babkas. Let rise in a warm place 1 hour until dough reaches tops of pans. Preheat oven to 350°F (175°C). Bake 40 minutes until babkas sound hollow when tapped on top. Remove from pans. Cool at least 30 minutes. Serve immediately sprinkled with powdered sugar or wrap in heavy foil and freeze. Makes 2 loaves.

Lemon-Cheese Filling:
Place cream cheese and cottage cheese in a small bowl. Beat until smooth. Beat in egg yolk and sugar. Stir in lemon peel.

Nut Topping:
Place all ingredients in a small bowl. Toss with 2 forks until crumbs form.

Polka Dot Quick Bread *Photo on page 111.*

Frozen cranberries are easier to cut if they still have ice crystals in them.

2 cups fresh or frozen cranberries
1 cup milk
1 egg, slightly beaten
1/4 cup butter or margarine, melted
1 tablespoon grated orange peel
2 cups all-purpose flour

1 cup sugar
1 tablespoon baking powder
1/2 teaspoon salt
1-1/2 cups shredded mellow Cheddar cheese
  (6 oz.)
1/2 cup coarsely chopped walnuts

Preheat oven to 350°F (175°C). Grease a 9" x 5" loaf pan; set aside. Cut cranberries in half; set aside. In a medium bowl, combine milk, egg, butter or margarine and orange peel. Set aside. Sift flour, sugar, baking powder and salt into a large bowl. Add halved cranberries, cheese and nuts. Toss with a fork to distribute. Add milk mixture all at once. Stir until flour mixture is just moistened. Turn into prepared pan. Bake 1 hour 15 minutes in preheated oven until a wooden pick inserted in center comes out clean. Cool in pan on a rack 10 minutes. Remove from pan. Cool to room temperature on rack before slicing. Makes 1 loaf.

How to Make
Company Brunch Babkas

1/Press 1 piece of dough over bottom and 1/2-inch up side of each pan.

2/Cover filling with dough circle. To seal, press edges together with handle of wooden spoon.

Brasilianas

Store these and other soft cookies in a tightly covered container.

1 (14-oz.) can sweetened condensed milk
2 egg yolks
2 cups flaked coconut
2 cups finely chopped pecans

1/3 cup freshly grated Parmesan cheese (1 oz.)
1/2 cup sugar
2 teaspoons unsweetened cocoa powder
1 teaspoon instant coffee powder

Preheat oven to 325°F (165°C). Butter 2 baking sheets; set aside. Beat milk, egg yolks, coconut, pecans and cheese in a medium bowl until blended. Shape teaspoonfuls of dough into balls. Place 1 inch apart on prepared baking sheets. Bake 8 to 9 minutes in preheated oven until golden. Combine sugar, cocoa powder and coffee powder in a small bowl. Roll hot cookies in sugar mixture. Place on racks to cool. Makes 85 to 95 cookies.

Cream Cheese Frosting

Use this creamy topping to dress up any plain cake.

2 (3-oz.) pkgs. cream cheese,
   room temperature
1 (1-lb.) box powdered sugar, sifted

1 teaspoon vanilla extract
1 to 2 tablespoons milk

In a small bowl, beat cream cheese by hand or with electric mixer on medium speed until very soft and fluffy. Gradually beat in powdered sugar. Add vanilla and enough milk to make a good spreading consistency. Use to frost and fill an 8- or 9-inch layer cake. Makes about 2 cups.

Variations

Chocolate: Melt 2 (1-ounce) squares unsweetened baking chocolate. Add to beaten cream cheese. Increase milk to about 3 tablespoons.

Orange: Omit vanilla. Substitute orange juice for milk. Add 2 tablespoons grated orange peel.

Coffee: Add 1 tablespoon instant coffee powder with powdered sugar.

Mocha: Add 3 tablespoons unsweetened cocoa powder with powdered sugar. Substitute 3 to 4 tablespoons cooled strong coffee for the milk.

Sour Cream: Substitute 1/4 cup dairy sour cream for the milk.

Lemon: Omit vanilla. Add 2 teaspoons grated lemon peel. Before adding milk, add 1 tablespoon lemon juice. Add 1 to 2 additional teaspoons milk, if needed.

Maple-Nut: Substitute 1/2 teaspoon maple extract for the vanilla. Stir in 1/2 cup chopped walnuts. Add 1 to 2 additional teaspoons milk, if needed.

Coconut: Substitute canned coconut cream for the milk. If desired, sprinkle top of frosted cake with flaked or shredded coconut.

Cherry: Substitute juice from maraschino cherries for the milk. Substitute 1/4 teaspoon almond extract for the vanilla.

Raisin-Pecan: Prepare frosting as directed above. Fold in 1/2 cup chopped raisins and 1/2 cup chopped pecans. Add 1 to 2 additional teaspoons milk, if needed.

Sweet Pies

Imaginative cheese pies offer a nutritional bonus of protein that most desserts can't claim. Most of these pies are hearty—just right to round out a light meal. Sweet cheese pies add a fresh touch to a supper of leftovers and are perfect to offer guests who have been invited for dessert and coffee. All are handsome desserts you can make in advance—always an advantage when you are entertaining—and serve with justifiable pride.

When pie fillings are thickened with cornstarch, mix the cornstarch with other dry ingredients. Then add enough liquid to make a paste before adding the rest of the liquid. Cook starchy thickening agents such as cornstarch, flour or tapioca over medium to low heat. High temperature, long cooking and continuous stirring give a thinner and darker mixture because the starch cells rupture and brown. This is true for pie fillings, puddings or gravies.

The amount of moisture used in standard pie crusts is important if you want a tender flaky crust. If you use too little water, there won't be enough moisture to separate the layers and make them flaky. Too much water results in a crust that is dull and pale. Even though it's flaky, a too-moist crust is tough and shrinks from the pan.

Some sweet pies need a sweetened crust to be at their best. Sweetened Crumb Crust is made with cookie crumbs or graham cracker crumbs. Graham cracker crumbs are the most popular and are available in your supermarket. However, vanilla wafer crumbs give a milder flavored crust that is perfect for airy, chiffon pies. Chocolate cookie crumbs are used mainly with chocolate fillings.

If you're not serving a cheese pie tonight, the next best thing is a pie with a cut of cheese beside it. Cut the cheese into neat, eye-pleasing shapes—wedges, squares, triangles or cubes. Cheese is easier to cut and shred when it is cold, however, let the cheese come to room temperature before serving it with your favorite pie.

Valentine's Day Lunch
Little Beef & Blue Loaves, page 67
Roman Artichokes, page 93
Fresh Green Salad with French Dressing
Crescent Rolls
Sweetheart Tart, page 132

California Cottage Pie

You can make cookie crumbs by processing a few cookies at a time in your blender.

Sweetened Crumb Crust made with
   vanilla wafer cookie crumbs, page 129
1 tablespoon unflavored gelatin powder
1/2 cup sugar
3 eggs, separated
1/2 cup water

1 (6-oz.) can frozen orange juice
   concentrate, thawed
2 cups cream-style cottage cheese (1 lb.)
1/4 cup sugar
1 cup dairy sour cream
1 medium navel orange, thinly sliced

Preheat oven to 325°F (165°C). Prepare Sweetened Crumb Crust in a 9-inch pie pan. Bake 10 minutes. Cool 10 minutes on a rack; refrigerate. In a medium saucepan, combine gelatin powder and 1/2 cup sugar. Beat in egg yolks until combined. Stir in water and orange juice concentrate until blended. Stir constantly over medium heat until mixture comes to boiling point. Do not boil. Remove from heat. Cool 10 minutes. Press cottage cheese through a sieve into a medium bowl. Stir in cooled gelatin mixture until blended. Refrigerate until mixture mounds slightly when dropped from a spoon, about 30 minutes. In a medium bowl, beat egg whites with a wire whip or with electric mixer on medium speed until foamy. Gradually beat in 1/4 cup sugar until stiff peaks form. Fold egg whites, then sour cream, into chilled gelatin mixture. Spoon into prepared crust. Chill 2 hours or overnight. Cut orange slices in half. Garnish chilled pie with halved orange slices. Makes 6 servings.

How to Make Fruit Tarts

1/Place 1 slice of dough in bottom of cup. Overlap 5 slices around side; press together.

2/Spoon chilled filling into baked tart shells. Sprinkle with 1 tablespoon shredded cheese.

Sweetened Crumb Crust

For other crumb crusts, see individual cheesecake recipes, pages 137 to 146.

2 cups cookie crumbs or
  graham cracker crumbs
1/4 cup sugar

1/2 cup butter or margarine, melted
1/4 teaspoon ground cinnamon or
  ground nutmeg, if desired

In a medium bowl, use a fork or your fingers to combine all ingredients. Press into a 9-inch pie pan or a 9-inch springform pan, spreading evenly over bottom and up side. Do not attempt to make a high, fluted edge with this type of crust. To bake, place in a 325°F (165°C) oven for 10 minutes.

Variations

Nut Crust: Substitute 1/2 cup very finely chopped almonds, walnuts, pecans or peanuts for 1/2 cup of the crumbs.
Coffee Crust: Stir 1 tablespoon dry instant coffee powder into crumbs.

Fruit Tarts

When winter doldrums get you down, serve these for a taste of springtime.

Cheese Tart Shells, see below
2 navel oranges, peeled, sectioned
1 (8-1/4-oz.) can crushed pineapple
1/4 cup sugar
5 teaspoons cornstarch

1/8 teaspoon salt
1/2 cup orange juice
1 tablespoon lemon juice
3/4 cup shredded sharp Cheddar cheese (3 oz.)

Cheese Tart Shells:
1/2 cup vegetable shortening
1 (5-oz.) jar American cheese spread

1-1/2 cups all-purpose flour

Prepare Cheese Tart Shells; set aside. Cut each orange section into 3 pieces; set aside. Drain pineapple, reserving syrup. In a small saucepan, combine sugar, cornstarch and salt. Stir in reserved pineapple syrup, orange juice and lemon juice. Stir gently over medium heat until mixture thickens and bubbles. Stir in orange pieces and pineapple. Refrigerate 1 hour. Spoon chilled filling into baked tart shells. Sprinkle each tart with about 1 tablespoon Cheddar cheese. Makes 12 tarts.

Cheese Tart Shells:
Combine shortening and cheese spread in a medium bowl. Cut flour into cheese mixture with two knives until blended. Shape into a roll 1-1/4 inches in diameter and 12 inches long. Wrap completely in waxed paper or plastic wrap. Refrigerate 1 hour or more. Preheat oven to 375°F (190°C). Remove dough from refrigerator; unwrap. Slice 1/8-inch thick. Using twelve 2-3/4-inch muffin cups or 3-inch tart pans, place 1 slice of dough in bottom of each. Overlap 5 slices around outside of each. Gently press together. Prick bottoms and sides with a fork. Bake 18 to 20 minutes in preheated oven until lightly browned. Cool in pans on a rack. Carefully remove from pans.

Ricotta Nesselrode Pie

Use a vegetable peeler to cut chocolate curls from a cube of semisweet chocolate.

Orange-Almond Pastry, see below
2-1/2 cups ricotta cheese (1-1/4 lbs.)
1-1/3 cups granulated sugar
1 tablespoon all-purpose flour
4 eggs, slightly beaten
1 teaspoon rum extract

3 tablespoons chopped candied citron
3 tablespoons chopped candied orange peel
3 tablespoons coarsely chopped semisweet
   chocolate pieces
3 tablespoons powdered sugar, if desired
Chocolate curls

Orange-Almond Pastry:
1 (11-oz.) pkg. pie crust mix
2 teaspoons sugar
3 tablespoons very finely chopped
   toasted blanched almonds

2 tablespoons frozen orange juice
   concentrate, thawed
3 tablespoons cold water

Prepare Orange-Almond Pastry. On a lightly floured surface, roll out 1/2 of pastry to an 11-1/2-inch circle. Fit into a 10-inch glass pie pan or deep 9-inch metal pie pan. Gently trim edge 1/2 inch larger than pan. Roll out remaining pastry to a 10-inch square. Let dry slightly. Preheat oven to 350°F (175°C). In a large bowl, beat ricotta cheese, granulated sugar and flour with electric mixer on medium speed until smooth. Beat in eggs and rum extract until light and fluffy. Stir in citron, orange peel and chopped chocolate pieces. Spoon filling into prepared pastry shell. Cut slightly dry pastry into ten 10" x 1" strips. Weave strips evenly over filling to make a lattice top. Turn strips and bottom crust under even with edge of pie pan. Flute with fingers or press with tines of a fork. Bake 1 hour in preheated oven until pastry is golden and filling is firm. If pastry becomes brown too soon, place a 12-inch square of foil over pie and continue baking. Cool on a rack 30 minutes. Sprinkle with powdered sugar if desired. Top with chocolate curls. Makes 6 to 8 servings.

Orange-Almond Pastry:
In a medium bowl, combine pie crust mix, sugar and almonds. Combine orange juice concentrate and water in a small bowl. Gradually add to pie crust mixture, tossing with a fork to distribute evenly. Mixture should pack together when pressed into your palm.

Variation
Walnuts or pecans may be substituted for almonds in the pastry.

Updated Linzer Tart

Named for Linz, Austria, this open-face raspberry tart is like a jam pie.

1 (11-oz.) pkg. pie crust mix
1/3 cup finely chopped toasted almonds
Water
3/4 cup seedless red raspberry jam or
    preserves

1-3/4 cups shredded Swiss cheese (7 oz.)
3 eggs, slightly beaten
1 cup half-and-half or light cream
1/4 cup sugar
1/8 teaspoon salt

Preheat oven to 350°F (175°C). Butter a 9-inch springform pan; set aside. In a medium bowl, combine pie crust mix and almonds. Add water according to package directions. On a lightly floured surface, roll about 2/3 of the dough into a 12-inch circle. Gently fit into bottom and up side of prepared pan. Trim off excess dough. Cut remaining 1/3 of the dough into 8 pieces. With hands, roll each piece into a 9-inch rope; set aside. Carefully spread jam or preserves over bottom of pastry shell in pan. Sprinkle evenly with cheese. In a medium bowl, beat eggs, cream, sugar and salt. Pour evenly over cheese. Arrange ropes of pastry about 1 inch apart over filling, like spokes of a wheel. Pinch ends of ropes and bottom pastry together. Bake 35 to 40 minutes in preheated oven until golden brown and slightly puffed. Cool 10 minutes on a rack. Carefully remove side of pan. Cool to room temperature, about 20 minutes. Cut into wedges to serve. Makes 6 to 8 servings.

Sweetheart Tart

Glazed strawberries top an elegant cheese filling which hides a sweet surprise.

Standard Pastry for Cheese Pies,
    Single Crust, page 77
1/2 cup semisweet chocolate pieces
1 (8-oz.) pkg. cream cheese,
    room temperature
1 cup powdered sugar, sifted

1/2 cup heavy cream or whipping cream
1 tablespoon Grand Marnier
1/2 teaspoon vanilla extract
1/2 cup seedless red raspberry jam or
    preserves
1 qt. fresh strawberries, washed, hulled

Prepare and bake pastry shell in a 9-inch pie pan. Melt chocolate pieces in a small heavy saucepan over very low heat. Use a rubber spatula to spread melted chocolate evenly over bottom of cooled pastry shell. Let stand until chocolate is set, 10 to 15 minutes. In a large bowl, beat cheese with electric mixer until fluffy. Blend in powdered sugar. Increase speed to high and beat 1 minute longer. Blend in cream, Grand Marnier and vanilla. Spoon cheese mixture over chocolate layer in pastry shell. Refrigerate 30 minutes. Melt raspberry jam or preserves in a small heavy saucepan over low heat. Arrange strawberries over cheese filling, stem end down. Gently spoon melted jam or preserves over berries. Refrigerate at least 3 hours. Makes 6 to 8 servings.

When recipes call for unsweetened, semisweet *or* sweet *chocolate, use cooking chocolate, not chocolate candy.*

Grandma's Cheese Custard Pie

Lower the calorie count by substituting fresh fruit for the whipped cream topping.

Standard Pastry for Cheese Pies,
   Single Crust, page 77
1 cup dairy sour cream
1 cup shredded Swiss cheese (4 oz.)
4 eggs
1/3 cup granulated sugar
1 tablespoon vanilla extract

2 cups milk
Grated nutmeg
1 cup heavy cream or whipping cream
2 tablespoons powdered sugar
2 (1-oz.) squares unsweetened baking
   chocolate, grated

Prepare pastry shell in a 9-inch pie pan; set aside. Preheat oven to 350°F (175°C). Combine sour cream and cheese in a 2-quart saucepan. Stir constantly over low heat until cheese melts. Do not boil. Remove from heat. Cool 20 minutes. Add eggs one at a time, beating well after each addition. Stir in granulated sugar and vanilla. Gradually beat in milk. Pour into prepared pastry shell. Sprinkle lightly with nutmeg. Bake about 40 minutes in preheated oven until browned and puffed. Cool on a rack 15 minutes. Refrigerate until served. Before serving, beat heavy cream or whipping cream with a wire whip until slightly thickened. Beat in powdered sugar. Fold in grated chocolate by hand. Spread whipped cream mixture over pie. Makes 6 servings.

How to Make Sweetheart Tart

1/Spoon cream cheese mixture evenly over cooled chocolate in pastry shell.

2/Carefully spoon melted jam or preserves over strawberries and chilled cheese mixture.

Chocolate Bliss

Melt chocolate in the top of a double boiler or in a small heavy pan over very low heat.

Chocolate Crumb Crust, see below
2 (8-oz.) pkgs. cream cheese,
   room temperature
3/4 cup firmly packed light brown sugar
1 teaspoon vanilla extract

6 (1-oz.) squares semisweet baking chocolate,
   melted
2 eggs
1/2 cup chopped toasted blanched almonds,
   if desired

Chocolate Crumb Crust:
2 cups chocolate cookie crumbs
1/4 cup sugar

1/2 cup butter or margarine, melted
1/4 teaspoon ground cinnamon, if desired

Prepare Chocolate Crumb Crust; set aside. Preheat oven to 325°F (165°C). In a large bowl, beat cream cheese, sugar and vanilla until blended. Beat in melted chocolate. Add eggs one at a time, beating well after each addition. Pour into prepared crust. Bake 35 minutes in preheated oven. Refrigerate 6 hours. Sprinkle with chopped almonds. Cut into wedges. Makes 6 servings.

Chocolate Crumb Crust:
Combine all ingredients in a medium bowl. Press evenly over bottom and side of a 9-inch pie pan.

Swiss Apple Pie

After trying this one, you'll want to put cheese in other traditional pies.

1-3/4 cups shredded Swiss cheese (7 oz.)
1 (11-oz.) pkg. pie crust mix
Cold water
1/2 cup firmly packed light brown sugar
1/8 teaspoon ground cinnamon
1/8 teaspoon ground cloves
1/8 teaspoon ground nutmeg

1/8 teaspoon salt
6 medium cooking apples, peeled, cored,
   thinly sliced
2 tablespoons butter or margarine
1 tablespoon lemon juice
1/2 teaspoon grated lemon peel
4 oz. Swiss cheese, finely diced

In a medium bowl, use 2 forks to toss shredded cheese with pie crust mix. Add cold water according to package directions. Divide into 2 parts, making 1 slightly larger than the other. Wrap separately in foil or plastic wrap. Refrigerate 20 minutes. On a lightly floured surface, roll out larger piece of pastry to an 11-inch circle. Fit into a 9-inch pie pan. Trim edge 1/2 inch larger than pan; set aside. Preheat oven to 450°F (230°C). In a large bowl, combine brown sugar, cinnamon, cloves, nutmeg and salt. Add apples, tossing gently until coated with brown sugar mixture. Turn into prepared pastry shell. Drop pieces of butter or margarine evenly over filling. Sprinkle filling evenly with lemon juice, lemon peel and diced cheese. Roll out remaining pastry. Make several small cuts to let steam escape during baking. Lift top pastry with rolling pin and center over filling. Remove rolling pin. Trim edge 1/2 inch larger than pan. Flute edge with your fingers or turn under and press with tines of a fork dipped in flour. Bake 10 minutes in preheated oven. Reduce heat to 375°F (190°C). Bake about 1 hour longer until apples are tender. Cool on a rack. Makes 6 to 8 servings.

Better-Than-Ever Pumpkin Pie

If you use home canned or frozen pumpkin, drain it well before you measure it.

Standard Pastry for Cheese Pies,
  Single-Crust, page 77
1-1/2 cups cream-style cottage cheese (12 oz.)
1 tablespoon frozen orange juice
  concentrate, thawed
1-1/2 cups canned pumpkin
3 eggs

3/4 cup sugar
1 teaspoon ground cinnamon
1/2 teaspoon ground ginger
1/2 teaspoon ground allspice
1/4 teaspoon ground cloves
Whipped cream, if desired

Prepare pastry shell in a 9-inch pie pan; set aside. Preheat oven to 350°F (175°C). In blender, process cottage cheese and orange juice concentrate on medium speed until smooth. Add pumpkin, eggs, sugar, cinnamon, ginger, allspice and cloves. Process on medium speed about 2 minutes. Pour into pastry shell. Bake about 1 hour in preheated oven until a knife inserted in center of pie comes out clean. Cool on a rack 15 minutes. Refrigerate until served. Top individual servings with whipped cream, if desired. Makes 6 to 8 servings.

Cheese Garnishes for Pies

Creamy cheese toppings, miniature cheese apples, and spicy cheese sauces will add flavor and cheer to your favorite pies.

Gingered Cheese Topping:
Beat 2 (3-ounce) packages room temperature cream cheese until fluffy. Gradually beat in 1 cup powdered sugar until smooth. Beat in 5 tablespoons half-and-half or light cream. Gently stir in 2 tablespoons finely chopped candied ginger. Spoon over juicy fruit pies.

Edam-Pecan Topping:
Crumble 3/4 pound room temperature Edam cheese into a medium bowl. Add 1/2 cup coarsely chopped pecans and 1 cup half-and-half or light cream. Beat until fluffy. Spoon over pumpkin, mince and apple pies. Top with pecan halves.

Easy Topping:
About 5 minutes before apple or cherry pies are done, place wedge-shaped slices of mild, mellow or sharp Cheddar cheese on top. Return to oven to complete baking.

Cheddar Sauce:
Place 1-1/4 cups shredded sharp Cheddar cheese in the top of a double boiler. Add 1/2 cup half-and-half or light cream and 2 drops hot pepper sauce. Stir frequently over simmering water until mixture is smooth. Spoon over any fruit pie.

Little Cheese Apples:
In a medium bowl, toss 2 cups shredded Gruyere cheese with 1 tablespoon heavy cream or whipping cream. Shape cheese mixture into balls about the size of walnuts. Add about 1 teaspoon additional cream if cheese balls do not hold shape. Insert 1 whole clove into one side and a small strip of angelica into the opposite side of each ball to represent the blossom and stem ends of an apple. Dip one cheek of each cheese apple into paprika. Refrigerate and serve with holiday pies.

Cheesecakes

Cheesecakes have been with us a long time. A big, handsome cheesecake—probably garnished with fruit—was the favorite birthday cake during the days of the Holy Roman Empire. It was also a delicacy during the reign of Elizabeth I in England. In Eighteenth Century Great Britain and her colonies, cheesecake usually graced the dessert table—a separate meal served in the homes of the wealthy and high-born.

Cheesecakes can be made in pie pans, round or square cake pans, ring molds, tube pans, cheesecake pans or springform pans. Cheesecake pans are round, 9 inches deep and have a removable bottom. Springform pans are round, 8, 9 or 10 inches deep and have a side equipped with a buckle for easy removal. After baking a cheesecake in a springform pan, run the blade of a thin knife around the side of the pan to loosen the baked crust. To prevent the crust from collapsing, wait until the cheesecake is completely cooled before removing the side of the pan.

The filling of a baked cheesecake should be firm enough so a knife inserted off-center comes out clean. The surface will be dry, but soft and spongy to touch. When a baking time range is given, test the filling at the earliest time given, then test once or twice again until the final time.

If your cheesecake cracks and falls somewhat, rest assured that it's not a failing of the cook, but the nature of cheesecakes. To reduce the extent of falling and cracking, cool cheesecakes very slowly. The easiest way is to turn the oven off, leaving the cheesecake in the oven two to three hours. When the oven reaches room temperature, remove the cheesecake. No matter what you do, the dense, rather dry versions sink as they cool and usually develop a crack in the center.

Happily, cheesecakes are make-aheads—great when you entertain. They keep well up to a week in the refrigerator. Cover the cheesecake with a tent of foil or with a large hard plastic cover that allows a small amount of air space. Too much air will dry the cake. You can freeze most cheesecakes two to three months. Chill the cheesecake in the refrigerator, then wrap it completely with heavy foil before freezing. Thaw the cheesecake in the refrigerator eight to twelve hours. Its texture will be slightly more grainy than the freshly baked product but will still be acceptable.

Dessert Buffet

Big-Production Mocha Cheesecake, page 137
Celebration Cake, page 120
Cold Lime Soufflé
Strawberries en Chemise, page 148

Big-Production Mocha Cheesecake

When you whip cream, be careful not to get it too stiff or it will turn to butter.

Coco-Crumb Crust, see below
4 (3-oz.) pkgs. cream cheese,
   room temperature
3/4 cup sugar
2 eggs
1 tablespoon coffee-flavored liqueur
1 teaspoon vanilla extract
1 cup dairy sour cream

1 (1-oz.) square unsweetened baking
   chocolate, grated
Mocha Crown, see below
1 cup heavy cream or whipping cream,
   whipped
3/4 cup toasted sliced blanched almonds

Coco-Crumb Crust:
1-1/3 cups graham cracker crumbs
3 tablespoons sugar

3 tablespoons unsweetened cocoa powder
1/3 cup butter or margarine, melted

Mocha Crown:
1-1/2 teaspoons instant coffee powder
2 tablespoons boiling water
4 (1-oz.) squares semisweet baking chocolate
4 eggs, separated

1/3 cup sugar
1 tablespoon coffee-flavored liqueur or rum
1/2 teaspoon vanilla extract

Prepare and bake Coco-Crumb Crust. Place on a rack to cool. Do not turn off oven. In a large bowl, beat cream cheese with electric mixer on high speed until light and fluffy. Gradually beat in sugar. Add eggs 1 at a time, beating well after each addition. Add liqueur and vanilla. Turn into prepared crust. Bake 30 minutes in preheated oven. Cool on a rack 10 minutes. Gently spread sour cream over cheesecake. Sprinkle with grated chocolate. Refrigerate 30 minutes. Prepare Mocha Crown. Gently spread Mocha Crown over refrigerated cheesecake. Refrigerate until firm, 2 to 3 hours. Loosen and remove side of pan. Place cheesecake on a serving plate. Spoon whipped cream over top of cake. Sprinkle almonds around edge. Makes 12 servings.

Coco-Crumb Crust:
Preheat oven to 350°F (175°C). In a medium bowl, combine crumbs, sugar, cocoa powder and butter or margarine. Press mixture firmly on bottom and up side of a 9-inch springform pan. Bake 10 minutes in preheated oven.

Mocha Crown:
In top of double boiler over hot but not boiling water, dissolve coffee powder in 2 tablespoons boiling water. Add chocolate, stirring until chocolate is melted and mixture is blended. Remove from heat. In a medium bowl, beat egg whites with electric mixer until stiff; set aside. Beat egg yolks in a large bowl until thick and pale. Gradually beat in sugar. Add chocolate mixture about 1/4 cup at a time, beating well after each addition. Beat in coffee-flavored liqueur or rum and vanilla. Gently fold in beaten egg whites by hand.

Chocolate will melt without burning or separating if you heat it in the top of a double boiler over hot water.

Fruited Cheesecake Austrian-Style

You don't usually think of Swiss cheese when you think of cheesecake, but this is delicious.

Sweetened Crumb Crust made with
 graham cracker crumbs, page 129
3 cups dairy sour cream
4 cups shredded Swiss cheese (16 oz.)
1-1/2 cups sugar
1/4 cup all-purpose flour

2 tablespoons grated orange peel
6 eggs
1 pint fresh strawberries, hulled
1/2 cup well-drained pineapple chunks
1/2 cup red currant jelly

Prepare Sweetened Crumb Crust in a 9-inch springform pan. Leave 1/2 inch around top of pan uncovered. Set aside; do not bake. Combine sour cream and Swiss cheese in a medium saucepan. Stir constantly over very low heat until cheese is melted. Do not boil. Gradually stir in sugar until dissolved. Remove from heat. Cool 20 minutes on a rack. Preheat oven to 350°F (175°C). Turn cheese mixture into a large bowl. Gradually beat in flour and orange peel with electric mixer on medium speed. Add eggs one at a time, beating well after each addition. Pour into prepared crumb crust. Bake 40 to 50 minutes in preheated oven until filling is set and lightly browned. Cool 10 minutes on a rack. Refrigerate 2 hours. Remove side of pan. Slice strawberries lengthwise. Cut pineapple chunks into fourths. Before serving, arrange strawberries and pineapple on top of cheesecake. In a small saucepan over low heat, stir jelly until melted. Cool slightly. Spoon jelly over strawberries. Let stand at room temperature about 10 minutes until jelly sets. Makes 10 servings.

Bourbon Street Cheesecake

Ever taste a New Orleans praline? That's the flavor captured in this heavenly dessert.

Sweetened Crumb Crust made with
 graham cracker crumbs, page 129
3 (8-oz.) pkgs. cream cheese, room
 temperature
1-1/4 cups firmly packed dark brown sugar
2 tablespoons all-purpose flour

3 eggs
1-1/2 teaspoons vanilla extract
1/2 cup finely chopped pecans
2 tablespoons liquid brown sugar
12 pecan halves

Preheat oven to 325°F (165°C). Prepare Sweetened Crumb Crust in a 9-inch springform pan. Bake 10 minutes in preheated oven. Cool on a rack. Do not turn off oven. In a large bowl, beat cream cheese, dark brown sugar and flour with electric mixer on medium speed until blended. Add eggs one at a time, beating well after each addition. At low speed, beat in vanilla. Stir in chopped pecans by hand. Gently pour mixture into prepared crust. Bake 50 to 55 minutes in preheated oven until a knife inserted in center comes out clean. Cool on a rack 5 minutes. Use a thin knife to loosen crust from side of pan. Do not remove side of pan. Cool on a rack 30 minutes. Remove side of pan. Refrigerate at least 2 hours. To serve, brush top of cheesecake with liquid brown sugar. Decorate with pecan halves around edge. Cut in wedges. Makes 10 to 12 servings.

Old-Fashioned Cheesecake

This is the grande dame *of cheesecakes—big, rich, almost indescribably delicious.*

Butter Crust, see below
5 (8-oz.) pkgs. cream cheese,
   room temperature
1-1/2 cups sugar
1/4 cup all-purpose flour
2 teaspoons grated lemon peel
1/2 teaspoon salt

1/2 teaspoon ground nutmeg
1 tablespoon vanilla extract
6 eggs
1/2 cup heavy cream or whipping cream
Sour Cream Topping, see below
1 qt. fresh strawberries, hulled, cut in half

Butter Crust:
1-1/2 cups all-purpose flour
3 tablespoons sugar
2/3 cup cold butter or margarine

1 egg
1/4 teaspoon vanilla extract

Sour Cream Topping:
1-1/2 cups dairy sour cream
3 tablespoons sugar

1 tablespoon brandy

Prepare Butter Crust; set aside. Reduce oven temperature to 325°F (165°C). In a large bowl, beat cream cheese by hand or with electric mixer on medium speed until smooth and fluffy. In a small bowl, stir sugar, flour, lemon peel, salt and nutmeg to combine. Gradually blend flour mixture into beaten cream cheese. Blend vanilla and eggs in a small bowl. Slowly beat egg mixture into cheese mixture until just blended. Stir in cream until just blended. Pour evenly into prepared Butter Crust. Smooth top with the back of a spoon. Bake 1-1/4 hours in preheated oven until a knife inserted halfway between center and edge comes out clean. While cheesecake bakes, prepare Sour Cream Topping. Remove cheesecake from oven. Turn off heat. Spread topping over cheesecake. Leaving oven door ajar several inches, return cheesecake to oven for 1 hour to slowly cool. Place on a rack on counter to cool 15 minutes. Use the blade of a thin knife to loosen crust from side of pan. Do not remove side of pan. Cover and refrigerate until chilled, about 1 hour. Remove pan side. Return to refrigerator until served. To serve, spoon strawberries over cheesecake. Makes 18 to 20 servings.

Butter Crust:
Preheat oven to 400°F (205°C). Combine flour and sugar in a small bowl. With a pastry blender or 2 knives, cut in butter or margarine until crumbs are the size of small peas. In a second small bowl, beat egg and vanilla. Stir into flour mixture until a smooth ball forms. Press half of pastry over bottom of a 9-inch springform pan. Bake bottom crust 8 minutes in preheated oven. Cool on a rack 10 minutes. Grease side of springform pan. Fasten in place. Press remaining pastry around side of pan, touching baked bottom crust.

Sour Cream Topping:
Combine all ingredients in a small bowl.

Use oil to grease pans only when the food covers the entire pan. Exposed oil becomes brown and gummy and is hard to remove.

Festive Pumpkin Cheesecake

Springform pans come in various sizes. You'll need a 9-inch pan for this recipe.

Cinnamon-Crumb Crust, from Old-World
    Raisin Cheesecake, page 146
3 (8-oz.) pkgs. cream cheese,
    room temperature
3/4 cup granulated sugar
3/4 cup firmly packed light brown sugar
3 eggs

1 (1-lb.) can pumpkin
1 teaspoon ground cinnamon
1/2 teaspoon ground nutmeg
1/4 teaspoon ground cloves
1/4 teaspoon salt
1/4 cup heavy cream or whipping cream
Nut Topper, see below

Nut Topper:
6 tablespoons butter or margarine, room
    temperature

1 cup firmly packed light brown sugar
1 cup coarsely chopped walnuts

Lightly butter a 9-inch springform pan. Prepare Cinnamon-Crumb Crust. Press into prepared spring-form pan; refrigerate. Preheat oven to 325°F (165°C). In a large bowl, beat cream cheese with electric mixer on medium speed until smooth. Gradually beat in granulated sugar and brown sugar until mixture is light and fluffy. Add eggs one at a time, beating well after each addition. At low speed, beat in pumpkin, cinnamon, nutmeg, cloves, salt and cream. Pour into prepared crust. Bake in preheated oven until a knife inserted in the center comes out clean, about 1 hour 35 minutes. Prepare Nut Topper. Gently spoon Nut Topper over baked cheesecake. Bake 10 minutes longer. Cool to room temperature on a rack. With a thin knife, loosen crust from pan. Do not remove side of pan. Refrigerate 6 hours or overnight. Gently remove side of pan. Let stand 20 minutes at room temperature before serving. Makes 16 to 18 servings.

Nut Topper:
In a small bowl, beat butter or margarine and brown sugar together. Stir in walnuts.

Make cornflake crumbs by processing cornflakes in the blender or crushing them in a plastic bag.

Cheesecakes

Mr. Jones' Back-Home Cheesecake

"Back home" is Wales, where this surprising cheddar-beer dessert is a favorite.

Zwieback Crust, see below
4 (8-oz.) pkgs. cream cheese, room
   temperature
2 cups shredded sharp Cheddar cheese (8 oz.)
1-3/4 cups sugar

3 tablespoons all-purpose flour
5 whole eggs
3 egg yolks
1/4 cup dark beer

Zwieback Crust:
1 (6-oz.) pkg. zwieback toast, crushed
3 tablespoons sugar

6 tablespoons butter or margarine, melted

Prepare Zwieback Crust; refrigerate. Preheat oven to 475°F (245°C). In a large bowl, beat cream cheese and Cheddar cheese with electric mixer on medium speed until smooth. Beat in sugar and flour until fluffy. Add whole eggs and egg yolks one at a time, beating well after each addition. Stir in beer by hand. Pour into prepared crust. Bake 12 minutes in preheated oven. Reduce oven temperature to 250°F (120°C). Bake 1-1/2 hours longer.Turn off oven heat. Leave cake in closed oven 1 hour. Cool to room temperature on a rack about 15 minutes. With blade of a thin knife, loosen crust from side of pan. Remove side of pan. Serve immediately or refrigerate until served. Makes 14 servings.

Zwieback Crust:
Lightly butter a 9-inch springform pan. In a small bowl, blend all ingredients. Press over bottom and part way up side of prepared pan.

Store leftover egg whites in the refrigerator 2 to 3 days in a container with a tight-fitting lid. Freeze extra egg whites in small freezer containers. Label the container with the number of egg whites it contains. Store frozen egg whites 6 to 8 months and use as soon as they are thawed.

Slimmer's Delight

This extra-light cheesecake will satisfy your sweet tooth but it is low in fat and calories.

1/4 cup sugar

2 envelopes unflavored gelatin powder

3 eggs, separated

1/4 teaspoon salt

1-1/2 cups skim milk

3 cups ricotta cheese (1-1/2 lbs.)

3 tablespoons orange juice

1 tablespoon lemon juice

2 teaspoons grated orange peel

1/2 teaspoon grated lemon peel

1 teaspoon vanilla extract

1/2 cup sugar

5 gingersnaps, crushed, if desired

Orange sections, if desired

Lightly oil ten 6-ounce custard cups or individual molds; set aside. In a medium bowl, combine 1/4 cup sugar and gelatin. Beat in egg yolks until pale. Beat in salt and milk until blended. Pour into top of double boiler. Stir constantly over hot but not boiling water until mixture coats a metal spoon, about 10 minutes. Remove from heat; set aside. Process ricotta cheese in blender until smooth. Stir processed ricotta cheese, orange juice, lemon juice, orange peel, lemon peel and vanilla into hot milk mixture. In a large bowl, beat egg whites until soft peaks form. Gradually beat in 1/2 cup sugar until stiff peaks form. Gently fold cheese mixture into stiffly beaten egg whites until just blended. Spoon into prepared custard cups or molds. Cover and refrigerate 6 hours or overnight. To serve, run a knife around molds. Invert molds onto individual dessert dishes. Shake gently; remove molds. Garnish with gingersnap crumbs and orange sections if desired. Makes 10 servings.

How to Make Slimmer's Delight

1/Stir sugar mixture over hot water until mixture thickens slightly and coats a metal spoon.

2/Invert mold onto dessert dish. Shake gently; remove mold. Garnish with crumbs and orange sections.

Lemon-Honey Cheesecake

If your honey has crystalized, you can melt it by putting the jar in warm water.

Gingersnap Crumb Crust, see below
3 cups ricotta cheese (1-1/2 lbs.)
4 eggs
3/4 cup honey

1 cup half-and-half or light cream
2 teaspoons vanilla extract
1/2 teaspoon salt
Citrus Sauce, see below

Gingersnap Crumb Crust:
2 cups gingersnap cookie crumbs
1/2 cup sugar

1/2 cup butter or margarine, melted

Citrus Sauce:
1 cup water
1-1/2 tablespoons cornstarch
6 tablespoons sugar
1/3 cup lemon juice

2 teaspoons grated lemon peel
1/4 teaspoon ground ginger
1/8 teaspoon salt

Prepare Gingersnap Crumb Crust; set aside. Preheat oven to 325°F (165°C). In a large bowl, beat ricotta cheese with electric mixer on medium speed until smooth and fluffy. Add eggs one at a time, beating well after each addition. Beat in honey, cream, vanilla and salt until blended. Gently pour into prepared crust. Bake 1-1/2 hours in preheated oven until filling is set. Cool on a rack 30 minutes. With the blade of a thin knife, loosen crust from side of pan. Remove pan side. Refrigerate cheesecake until served. Prepare Citrus Sauce. To serve, spoon warm sauce over wedges of cold cheesecake. Makes 12 to 14 servings.

Gingersnap Crumb Crust:
Combine crumbs and sugar in a medium bowl. Use a fork or fingers to blend butter or margarine into crumb mixture. Press over bottom and up side of a 9-inch springform pan.

Citrus Sauce:
In a heavy saucepan, gradually stir water into cornstarch until smooth. Stir over low heat until cornstarch is dissolved, about 5 minutes. Stir in remaining ingredients until blended. Increase heat to medium-low. Stir constantly until mixture is thickened and clear. Keep warm.

Egg yolks seldom turn lemon-colored no matter how long they are beaten. They become thick and pale.

Triple-Chocolate Paradise

Grandmother used to call this an ice-box cake.

18 ladyfingers, split lengthwise
1/4 cup Caramella liqueur
3/4 cup sugar
1/2 cup water
3 egg yolks
2 (8-oz.) pkgs. cream cheese,
    room temperature, cut in pieces
1/2 cup Caramella liqueur

8 (1-oz.) squares unsweetened baking
    chocolate, melted, cooled
5 (1-oz.) squares semisweet baking chocolate,
    melted, cooled
2 cups heavy cream or whipping cream,
    stiffly beaten
1 (6-oz.) pkg. semisweet chocolate pieces
    or 1 cup crushed English-style toffee

Lightly butter a 9-inch springform pan; set aside. Sprinkle ladyfingers with 1/4 cup liqueur. Line bottom and side of pan with ladyfingers. Stir sugar and water in a small heavy saucepan over medium heat until sugar dissolves. Attach a candy thermometer to side of pan. Without stirring, heat to 240°F (115°C). One teaspoonful of syrup dropped into very cold water will gather into a soft ball. While syrup cooks, beat egg yolks in a large bowl with electric mixer on high speed until pale and thick. Continue to beat egg yolks while adding hot syrup in a thin, steady stream. Beat 3 minutes longer. On medium speed, beat in cream cheese pieces one at a time. Beat in 1/2 cup liqueur, unsweetened chocolate and semisweet chocolate. By hand, stir in about 1/4 of the whipped cream. Fold in remaining whipped cream and chocolate pieces or crushed toffee. Gently spoon into prepared pan. Cover with foil or plastic wrap. Refrigerate at least 6 hours. To serve, remove pan side and place cake on a round serving dish. Makes 16 to 18 servings.

How to Make Triple-Chocolate Paradise

1/Line side and bottom of buttered springform pan with ladyfinger halves.

2/Gently spoon chocolate mixture into pan without disturbing ladyfingers.

Farm-Style Buttermilk Cheesecake

Use a regular 8-inch, round cake pan to bake this delicious and easy dessert.

2 eggs
2 cups Farm-Style Buttermilk Cheese,
   page 18, or 2 (8-oz.) pkgs. cream cheese
1 cup sugar
1 teaspoon grated lemon peel
3 tablespoons lemon juice

1/2 teaspoon salt
3/4 teaspoon vanilla extract
2 cups sliced fresh peaches or nectarines, or
   canned sliced peaches, drained
Ground nutmeg

Pour water 1/2 inch deep into a 13" x 9" baking dish. Place baking dish in oven. Preheat oven to 325°F (165°C). Generously butter an 8-inch, round cake pan; set aside. Combine eggs, Farm-Style Buttermilk Cheese or cream cheese, sugar, lemon peel, lemon juice, salt and vanilla in blender. Process on medium speed until mixture is smooth. Pour into prepared cake pan. Place cake pan in heated water in baking dish. Bake 45 to 50 minutes in preheated oven until a knife inserted in center comes out clean. Cool slightly on rack. Cover and refrigerate. To serve, cut in wedges and spoon fruit over top. Sprinkle lightly with nutmeg. Makes 6 to 8 servings.

Old-World Raisin Cheesecake

Originally a German bread, zwieback toast *is found with baby teething biscuits in the store.*

Cinnamon-Crumb Crust, see below
3 cups small-curd cottage cheese (1-1/2 lbs.)
4 eggs
1 cup sugar
1/2 teaspoon salt
2 teaspoons grated lemon peel
2 teaspoons vanilla extract

3/4 teaspoon almond extract
2 tablespoons all-purpose flour
1 cup half-and-half or light cream
3/4 cup raisins
1/2 cup toasted slivered blanched almonds
Ground cinnamon

Cinnamon-Crumb Crust:
1 (6-oz.) pkg. zwieback toast, crushed
1/4 cup sugar

1 teaspoon ground cinnamon
1/2 cup butter or margarine, melted

Prepare Cinnamon-Crumb Crust; set aside. Preheat oven to 325°F (165°C). Process cottage cheese in food processor or blender on medium speed until smooth; set aside. In a large bowl, beat eggs with electric mixer on medium speed until blended. Gradually beat in sugar until mixture is thick and pale. Beat in salt, lemon peel, vanilla and almond extract until blended. Beat in flour and processed cottage cheese. Stir in cream, raisins and almonds by hand. Pour into prepared crust. Sprinkle with cinnamon. Bake about 35 minutes in preheated oven until a knife inserted in center comes out clean. Cool on a rack to room temperature, about 30 minutes. Cut into squares. Serve immediately or refrigerate until served. Makes 12 to 15 servings.

Cinnamon-Crumb Crust:
Blend all ingredients. Press mixture firmly over bottom and up sides of a 13" x 9" baking dish.

Cheese, Fruit & Wine

The simplest yet most elegant dessert you can serve is cheese and fruit. It is suitable for any meal from a family supper to an elaborate company dinner. Many restaurants serve cheese and fruit boards after the meal. In France, cheese is served before the sweet dessert.

As you plan your next party use the helpful charts below. Have a supply of cheese and fruit in the refrigerator and a few bottles of wine waiting, and you're ready for your guests. Best of all, these combinations are simple to shop for, to prepare and to serve. By the time the guests arrive you'll be calm, unharried and ready to enjoy your own party.

The only other food needed is crackers or crusty French or Italian Bread—no sweets. Have cheese servers available and knives to cope with fruit that must be peeled or sectioned. Remove the cheeses from the refrigerator about an hour before serving so they will be at their flavor-best.

Offer dry white and rosé wines chilled but not ice cold and red wines at cool room temperature. Serve apertif and dessert wines chilled or not, as you prefer. Open white and sparkling wines just before serving and red wines one to three hours before serving. Plan on one bottle of wine for two to three guests or be guided by your knowledge of your friends' capacities.

Cheese & Fruit Dessert Boards

Serve:	With:
Neufchâtel, Bel Paese, provolone, Gorgonzola	comice pears, Golden Delicious apples, Ribier grapes, Spanish melon
Camembert, mellow Cheddar, Edam, Stilton	Jonathan apples, muscat grapes, greengage plums, white-fleshed peaches
brick, Swiss, primost, Liederkranz	apricots, red Delicious apples, Anjou pears, honeydew melon
Danish blue, Brie, sharp Cheddar, Boursault	Seckel pears, Bing cherries, Winesap apples, elephant heart plums
cream cheese, Gouda, Port Salut, Tilsit	nectarines, navel oranges, fresh pineapple spears, pre-served guava shells
Muenster, Gruyère, Monterey Jack, Limburger	Grimes Golden apples, cantaloupe wedges, Italian prune plums, Tokay grapes

Cheese & Wine Parties

Serve:	With:
mild to medium sharp cheeses: Boursault, double and triple crèmes, Brie, mild Cheddar or Colby	dry or cocktail sherries, dry vermouth, Madeira, Sauternes
medium cheeses that won't overpower wine: Edam, Monterey Jack, teleme, Muenster, Gouda, Colby, brick, Gruyère, Tilsit	white Burgundy, Chenin Blanc, Pinot Chardonnay, Chablis, Pinot Blanc, Riesling, rosé, Tokay, Pouilly Fuisse
medium-to-sharp cheeses: Cheddar, Swiss, Port Salut, fontina, provolone, Liederkranz, blue, Gorgonzola	red Burgundies or Bordeaux, Petite Sirah, Zinfandel, Cabernet Sauvignon, Pinot Noir, Barbera, Chianti
assertive cheeses: Bel Paese, Brie, medium to sharp Cheddar, Camembert, Stilton	tawney or ruby port, cream sherries, Madeira, fruit wines, champagne

Strawberries en Chemise

It will be easier to get a smooth fondant if you sift the powdered sugar.

2 pints large strawberries
2 (3-oz.) pkgs. cream cheese,
   room temperature
3 cups powdered sugar, sifted

2 egg yolks
2 tablespoons kirsch or cherry brandy
Milk, if desired

Wash strawberries under lukewarm running water. Do not hull. Dry gently with paper towels; set aside. Line a baking sheet with waxed paper; set aside. In a large bowl, beat cream cheese until light and fluffy. Beat in powdered sugar, egg yolks and kirsch or cherry brandy until fondant has a smooth dipping consistency. Fondant should not run from a spoon but fall slowly in large droplets. If too thick, add 1/8 teaspoon milk at a time, blending after each addition. Holding berries by stem end, dip bottom half of each berry into fondant. Place on prepared baking sheet. Refrigerate until firm. Makes 6 servings.

Gjetost Baked Apples

The flavor of these apple slices will remind you of caramel apples.

6 Golden Delicious apples, peeled, cored
3 cups shredded gjetost cheese (12 oz.)

Preheat oven to 350°F (175°C). Lightly butter six 10-ounce custard cups; set aside. Cut apples crosswise into 1/4-inch slices. Place bottom slice of each apple into prepared custard cups. Sprinkle with about 1 tablespoon cheese. Continue layering apple slices and cheese until all are used. Sprinkle remaining cheese evenly over tops of apples. Place custard cups on a baking sheet. Bake about 25 minutes in preheated oven until apples are crisp-tender and cheese is melted. Serve immediately. Makes 6 servings.

Raspberries & Cream Mold

Superfine is an extra-fine granulated sugar that dissolves faster than regular sugar.

2 cups cream-style cottage cheese (1 lb.)
2 tablespoons lemon juice
1 cup superfine granulated sugar

2 cups dairy sour cream
1 (10-oz.) pkg. frozen raspberries,
   partially thawed

Process cottage cheese in blender on medium speed until smooth. Add lemon juice and superfine granulated sugar. Blend until combined. Fold in sour cream by hand. Turn into refrigerator tray. Freeze until firm, about 2 hours. With a knife, cut lengthwise through center of frozen cheese mixture. Cut twice crosswise to make 6 equal rectangles. Serve on 6 individual serving dishes. Top with raspberries. Makes 6 servings.

Cheddar Broiled Grapefruit

Grapefruit lasts only a few days at room temperature and up to a month in the refrigerator.

3 grapefruit, halved
3/4 cup shredded sharp Cheddar cheese
  (3 oz.)
1/2 cup firmly packed light brown sugar

1/4 teaspoon ground nutmeg
1/8 teaspoon salt
1/2 cup dairy sour cream
6 maraschino cherries

Preheat broiler. Use a grapefruit knife or kitchen shears to remove cores from grapefruit. Use a sharp knife to cut around sections. Place grapefruit on a baking sheet. Broil 4 inches from heat, 2 minutes. In a small bowl, toss cheese and brown sugar to combine. Sprinkle evenly over broiled grapefruit. Return grapefruit to broiler until cheese mixture melts and bubbles. Stir nutmeg and salt into sour cream. Top each grapefruit half with a dollop of the sour cream mixture. Return to broiler to glaze, about 30 seconds. Garnish with cherries. Makes 6 servings.

Variation

Substitute shredded Swiss or Gruyère cheese for the Cheddar cheese.
Substitute walnut or pecan halves for the maraschino cherries.

How to Make
Cheddar Broiled Grapefruit

1/Use scissors to remove cores from grapefruit.

2/Top broiled grapefruit with a dollop of sour cream.

Gorgonzola Pears

The pears will hold together and stand up better if they are not cored.

3 oz. Gorgonzola cheese
1 tablespoon brandy
4 ripe Bartlett pears
2 tablespoons lemon juice
1 (3-oz.) pkg. cream cheese,
 room temperature

1/3 cup dairy sour cream
4 tablespoons coarsely chopped pecans
4 whole cloves
4 sprigs fresh mint

In a small bowl, use a fork to blend Gorgonzola cheese and brandy until smooth. Set aside 15 minutes. Peel pears and cut in half. Brush all surfaces of pear halves with lemon juice; set aside. Beat cream cheese into Gorgonzola cheese mixture until smooth. Fold in sour cream. Spread 1/4 of the cheese mixture on 4 pear halves. Top with remaining pear halves. Filling will push out around edges. Press chopped pecans into filling. Stand pears large-end down on a serving dish. Top each pear with a whole clove to represent the stem and a mint sprig to represent leaves. Serve at once or cover with foil or plastic wrap and refrigerate no longer than 3 hours before serving. Makes 4 servings.

French Cream with Spiced Peach Compote

For individual servings, spoon the cheese mixture into 4-ounce molds.

1 cup dairy sour cream
1 cup heavy cream or whipping cream
3/4 cup superfine granulated sugar
1/4 cup water
1 tablespoon unflavored gelatin powder

1 (8-oz.) pkg. cream cheese,
 room temperature
1/2 teaspoon vanilla extract
Spiced Peach Compote, see below

Spiced Peach Compote:
2 (17-oz.) cans sliced peaches
1/2 cup golden raisins
1/4 cup firmly packed dark brown sugar

1/4 teaspoon ground nutmeg
1/8 teaspoon ground cloves

Lightly oil a 4-cup decorative mold; set aside. In a medium saucepan, combine sour cream and heavy cream or whipping cream. Stir in sugar. Stir over very low heat until sugar dissolves. Pour water into a small saucepan. Sprinkle gelatin powder over water. Let stand 5 minutes. Stir gelatin mixture over low heat until dissolved. Stir gelatin mixture into warm cream mixture. Remove from heat. In a small bowl, beat cream cheese with a wire whisk or with electric mixer on medium speed until very soft and fluffy. Reduce mixer speed to low. Gradually beat in cream mixture and vanilla until blended. Pour into prepared mold. Refrigerate at least 4 hours. Prepare Spiced Peach Compote. To serve, invert mold into a shallow bowl. Remove mold. Spoon chilled compote around molded cheese mixture. Serve immediately or refrigerate until served. Makes 8 servings.

Spiced Peach Compote:
Drain syrup from peaches into a small saucepan. Reserve peaches. Add raisins, brown sugar, nutmeg and cloves to peach syrup. Stir constantly over medium heat until sugar is dissolved. Gently stir in peaches. Refrigerate at least 1 hour.

Exquisite Stuffed Cherries

Fresh cherries are available in mid-summer, but you can buy dates and prunes all year.

32 fresh large Bing cherries
1 (3-oz.) pkg. cream cheese,
  room temperature
1/4 cup crumbled blue cheese (1 oz.)

Heavy cream or whipping cream
Fresh grape leaves, nasturtium leaves or
  gardenia leaves, washed, dried
1/4 cup slivered salted almonds

Remove stems from cherries. Discard stems. Rinse cherries in cool water. Dry on paper towels. Halve and pit cherries; set aside. In a small bowl, blend cream cheese and blue cheese with a fork until smooth. Add cream a few drops at a time until mixture is thin enough to spread. Mixture will still be quite stiff. Place 1 scant teaspoonful of the cheese mixture on a cherry half. Top with other half of cherry. Repeat with remaining cherries and cheese mixture. Arrange leaves on 4 dessert plates. Place 8 cherries on each plate. Sprinkle with about 1 tablespoon almonds. Makes 4 servings.

Variation

When fresh cherries are not in season, use cheese mixture to stuff 24 pitted dates (6 per serving) or 20 uncooked prunes (5 per serving).

Crema al Mascarpone

Mascarpone *is an uncured cheese similar to ricotta cheese.*

1 lb. fresh mascarpone cheese
1/2 cup sugar
4 eggs, separated

1/2 cup golden rum
1/2 cup coarsely chopped filberts
Assorted in season fresh fruits, if desired

In a medium bowl, use a fork to blend cheese and sugar until mixture is smooth. Beat in 1 egg yolk at a time until smooth. Stir in rum. In another medium bowl, beat egg whites with a wire whip until soft peaks form. Fold beaten egg whites into cheese mixture. Spoon into individual serving dishes. Chill at least 4 hours. Sprinkle with chopped filberts. Serve as a pudding or as a spread with assorted fruits, if desired. Makes 6 servings.

Variation

Substitute 1/2 cup orange juice and 1/8 teaspoon vanilla extract for the rum.

Cheeses pictured clockwise from top right: Jarlsberg, sharp Cheddar, Liederkranz, Colby.

Winter Gold

French Grand Marnier, *pronounced grawn-marn-YEA, is an orange-flavored brandy.*

4 cups shredded sharp Cheddar cheese,
   room temperature (1 lb.)
2 (3-oz.) pkgs. cream cheese,
   room temperature
1/4 cup butter or margarine,
   room temperature

6 tablespoons Grand Marnier
1 teaspoon dry mustard
1/8 teaspoon cayenne pepper
1/4 cup chopped candied orange peel
4 large Navel oranges, peeled, sectioned

In a medium bowl, beat Cheddar cheese, cream cheese, butter or margarine, Grand Marnier, dry mustard and cayenne pepper until blended. Lightly oil a 4-cup mold. Pack cheese mixture into mold. Cover with foil or plastic wrap. Refrigerate at least 4 hours. Invert mold onto a serving plate or small platter; remove mold. Garnish top of molded cheese with candied orange peel. Arrange orange sections around molded cheese. To serve, use small knives or spreaders to spread cheese mixture over orange sections. Makes 10 to 12 servings.

Roquefort-Stuffed Baked Pears

This lovely cold-weather dessert is best served hot.

6 winter nelis or large Seckel pears,
   peeled, halved, cored
Granulated sugar
Ground nutmeg
1 cup dry white wine
2 tablespoons Cognac

1/2 cup crumbled Roquefort cheese (2 oz.)
1/3 cup zwieback crumbs
1/3 cup chopped pecans
2 tablespoons butter or margarine,
   room temperature

Preheat oven to 350°F (175°C). Place pears cut-side up in a shallow baking dish. Sprinkle lightly with sugar and nutmeg. Combine wine and Cognac. Pour into pan around pears. Cover and bake 40 to 45 minutes until pears are tender. While pears bake, blend cheese, crumbs, pecans and butter or margarine. Remove cover from pears. Sprinkle cheese mixture evenly over pears. Bake uncovered 10 minutes longer. Serve hot with pan juices spooned over pears. Makes 6 servings.

Superfine sugar dissolves faster than granulated sugar. Use it in uncooked mixtures and for sweetening fruit.

Coeur à la Crème

A fine-mesh sieve will work nicely if you don't have a wicker or porcelain mold.

2 cups cream-style cottage cheese (1 lb.)
2 (8-oz.) pkgs. cream cheese,
    room temperature
1/8 teaspoon salt
2 cups heavy cream or whipping cream

About 3 cups whole strawberries, raspberries,
    sliced peaches, nectarines, pineapple or
    a combination of fruits; or 1-1/2 cups
    whole-fruit strawberry preserves
Granulated white or brown sugar, if desired

In a large bowl, beat cottage cheese, cream cheese and salt by hand or with electric mixer on low speed until smooth. Gradually beat in cream until mixture is smooth. Increase mixer speed to medium. Beat 1 minute longer. Cut 2 layers of cheesecloth 12 inches square. Rinse in cold water. Wring out excess water. Line a coeur à la crème basket or other pierced mold with wet cheesecloth. Pack cheese mixture into mold. Fold cheesecloth over cheese. Place mold in a shallow medium bowl. Refrigerate 8 hours or overnight. Discard whey. Turn back cheesecloth from top of cheese. Invert mold onto a platter. Remove mold. Carefully remove cheesecloth. To serve, arrange fruit on platter around molded cheese. Sprinkle with sugar if desired. Makes 8 to 10 servings.

How to Make Coeur à la Crème

1/Line a coeur à la crème basket or other mold with cheesecloth. Pack cheese mixture into mold.

2/Invert mold onto a platter. Remove mold and cheesecloth. Surround cheese with fruit.

Ginger-Honey Mound

Seedless grapes are usually called for in recipes because grape seeds are bitter.

1 cup Rich Cream-Style Cheese, page 16,
   or 1(8-oz.) pkg. cream cheese
2 tablespoons honey
4 teaspoons finely chopped candied ginger

Fresh green grape leaves
Seedless green grapes,
   broken into small bunches

In a small bowl, blend cheese, honey and ginger. Place cheese mixture in a small bowl with an airtight cover. Refrigerate at least 4 hours. To serve, arrange grape leaves on a serving plate. Mound cheese mixture in center of leaves. Surround with grape clusters. Makes about 1 cup.

Spice & Brandy Blend

Tart persimmons will offset the sweetness of the cheese dessert.

1 cup Rich Cream-Style Cheese, page 16,
   or 1 (8-oz.) pkg. cream cheese
2 tablespoons powdered sugar
1 tablespoon brandy

1/4 teaspoon ground cinnamon
1/2 cup small coffee-bean candies, if desired
Persimmon wedges or cantaloupe wedges,
   if desired

In a small bowl, blend cheese, powdered sugar, brandy and cinnamon. Cover with foil or plastic wrap to make an airtight seal. Refrigerate at least 4 hours. To serve, mound cheese mixture on a small plate. Place candies, persimmon wedges or cantaloupe wedges on plate around cheese mound. Makes about 1 cup.

Fragrant Almond Mold

Geranium leaves make an imprint and leave a faint spicy fragrance on the cheese.

1 cup Rich Cream-Style Cheese, page 16,
   or 1 (8-oz.) pkg. cream cheese
2 tablespoons powdered sugar
1/4 teaspoon almond extract

2 teaspoons milk
1/2 cup chopped toasted blanched almonds
Fresh geranium leaves

In a small bowl, blend cheese, powdered sugar, almond extract and milk. Stir in almonds; set aside. Wash geranium leaves in cold water. Dry thoroughly on paper towels. Line a 2-cup mold or bowl with dry leaves, placing veined side in. Lightly pack cheese mixture into leaf-lined mold. Cover with foil or plastic wrap to make an airtight seal. Refrigerate at least 4 hours. To serve, invert mold onto a serving plate. Gently remove leaves. Rinse leaves in cold water. Dry on paper towels. Use leaves to garnish molded cheese. Makes about 1-1/2 cups.

Index

8.729488821527 48